FATHER

IS

SPEAKING

ISBN: 978-0-9899888-7-2

PRINTED IN THE UNITED STATES OF AMERICA
10 9 8 7 6 5 4 3 2 1

FATHER IS SPEAKING

Do You Know His Voice?

DR. JOHNNIE BLOUNT

BE THE WORD

Acknowledgments

Kayla Kennada

I believe this book will be a game changer for many people for generations to come. I grew up desiring to recognize the voice of my Father. Now that I can and have been sharing prophecy and Words of Knowledge and Wisdom for about fifty years, the Holy Spirit spoke to me to put in print how to recognize His Voice. I could not have done this without the help of Kayla, who has been my faithful friend and partner in ministry for over thirty years. As a bonus, she even taught me how to use my computer. Thank you, Kayla, for your time and patience.

Lori Badry

When this book was in disarray and we tried for some years to prepare it for publishing, I asked the Lord for help with this. When I met Lori Badry at a meet and greet, Holy Spirit spoke to me that she would help me with my book. And she did. She rearranged it so it would flow. Thank you, Lori, for all of your hard work in adding your professional touch. Now, so many people can enjoy it.

Mary Jo Gremling

To a woman of God who caused me to have confidence that I could write a book. Without her help I do not know if any of my books would be published. Thank you, Mary Jo, for helping me to fulfill what the Lord has called me to do.

Donis Blount

To my wife of forty-five years. Thank you, Donis, for being patient and supporting me in the ministry.

To the Reader

THIS BOOK HAS WRITTEN itself through the events of my life from early childhood to the present. As you read it, my hope is that you will begin to fully comprehend the importance of the Holy Spirit in your life. Each chapter begins with vocabulary words that will help create a better understanding while you read. At the end of each chapter, you will find questions to give you time to reflect upon what you have read. The Bible verses throughout this book will open your mind and heart to the concepts the Lord wants to teach you.

Now sit back and relax and prepare yourself for a more meaningful relationship with the Holy Spirit which will, in turn, bless your life and the lives of those around you!

Introduction

THE PURPOSE OF THIS BOOK is to create a desire in your heart to recognize the voice of your Heavenly Father and be led by His Spirit in order to fulfill your purpose here on earth.

As a child, I had a fear of not knowing what the Holy Spirit was saying to me. One day my granddaddy was sharing with me about Judgment Day and how I would be judged for what I did or didn't do on this earth. My spirit came to life. I had a desire to know the Holy Spirit from that moment!

Another time, I was lying in the cornfield behind my house, and I had a yearning that I didn't want to be just another ordinary person. My passion to know Father was strong, and I couldn't know Him if I couldn't hear Him. I knew Jesus said in the Word, "My sheep hear My voice," and I realized I didn't hear His voice, so I cried until I had no tears left and my head was pounding in pain. I couldn't sleep that night! I wanted to make sure I was walking in my Father's purpose and His will for my life. How could I know His purpose if I didn't know His voice? This hunger and thirst set me on a quest to where I am today.

Because I had learned to hear the voice of Holy Spirit and to follow Him, when I was a teenager, He prompted me to move to Kentucky. I left my home of poverty and began to prosper. He led me to a church that taught about the Kingdom rather than religion. My ministry changed and grew as I began to win souls by the thousands every year. The last year before I changed from pastoring a church to leading a ministry, we experienced five thousand souls giving their lives to Christ.

By being obedient to the direction of the Holy Spirit, I was able to literally save lives. My wife Donis, two of my sons, and some of my friends are alive today because I asked Holy Spirit what I should do and obeyed Him. Sadly, I know of one life that could have been saved had I realized at the time how crucial it was to obey Him immediately.

Once I could hear Holy Spirit speak to me, I began to operate in the nine spiritual gifts of the Holy Spirit. Now, I have established a Kingdom Academy that teaches about the Holy Spirit. If I hadn't learned to hear His voice, I would still be living as I grew up—in poverty and bound in religion. I wouldn't be where I am today. Today, I am fulfilling His purpose and His calling on my life. This has been one of my greatest accomplishments. I want you to have that same burning desire to hear Holy Spirit's voice! I want you to experience all that life has to offer you as you listen to His voice.

WORDS TO KNOW
Before Reading Chapter 1

Religion—Man's effort to reach God by trying to work from the outside, through joining organizations or churches, and through good works, traditions, denominations, and laws

Kingdom—You are born into the Kingdom by accepting Jesus Christ as your Lord and Savior. It starts in the heart and works its way outward. It is the government of heaven in operation on the earth.

Supernatural—The invisible power of God manifested in the natural world through man

God—The uncreated Supreme Being, without beginning or end. Judaism, Islam, and Christianity all proclaim belief in one God. Christianity alone affirms that God is a trinity—a "Tri-unity."

Trinity—The central mystery of the Christian faith; the fundamental teaching that there is only one God, revealed in three Persons: Father, Son, and Holy Spirit. Christians are baptized in the *name* of the Father, the Son, and the Holy Spirit, not in the *names* of, for there is only one God, revealed as three distinct Persons.

Father—The first person of the Trinity (God the Father, Jesus the Son, and the Holy Spirit), the Creator of everything seen and unseen, including mankind. Jesus revealed that God is Father not only in being the Creator; He is eternally Father in His relationship to His only Son (Matthew 11:27).

Jesus—The second person of the Trinity (God the Father, Jesus the Son, and the Holy Spirit); the only begotten Son of God; eternally begotten (not created) by the Father; the eternal object of the Father's love. He is the Word who became flesh, dwelt among us, was crucified, died, was buried, and rose again on the third day. He ascended into heaven and sits at the right of the Father. He is the only way of salvation.

Holy Spirit—The third person of the Trinity (God the Father, Jesus the Son, and the Holy Spirit), the Spirit of the Father who abides in us when we receive the gift of salvation. The Holy Spirit is the eternal expression of love between the Father and the Son. The love of the Father for the Son and the Son for the Father is so strong it is a *Person*: the Holy Spirit. The Spirit has always existed, without beginning or end. He is at work since creation by being "spoken through the prophets" and sent by the Father to the disciples after Jesus ascended into heaven to now be with them (us) and guide them (us) "into all truth" (John 16:13).

Repent—To change your mind and way of doing things

Concordance—An alphabetical index of all the words in the Bible and their definitions

Tangible voice—A physical voice heard by human ears

1

Father Wants to Fellowship With Us

My sheep listen to my voice;
I know them and they follow me.

JOHN 10:27 NKJV

When he has brought all his own sheep outside, he
walks on ahead of them, and the sheep follow him
because they know his voice and recognize his call.

JOHN 10:4 AMP

DO YOU HEAR GOD'S VOICE but don't recognize it? How can you follow Him if you don't recognize His voice? Religion blinds and confuses you so you don't recognize His voice.

I remember the presence of the Holy Spirit coming upon me as I was lying atop the chicken coop. It was a cold winter day, but I felt the warmth and peace of the Holy Spirit. At only eight years old, I asked Him why I was born. He spoke to me and said, "You are going to do great things on earth!" I didn't know how, but I knew in my heart that it was true.

The next time I experienced His presence, I was walking across the field from my grandmother's house on Christmas Eve. I was ten years old. The Holy Spirit spoke to me and said, "Something good is going to happen to you."

The most powerful spiritual moment I remember happened when I was sitting in study hall during my seventh grade year. My family had begun going to church several months prior, and they had all been saved. I tried several

I realized I was trying to become what I already was.

times to ask Jesus into my heart, but I didn't feel anything. I became angry at the Lord because He wouldn't save me. During study hall I asked Him, "What am I supposed to do to become saved?" His Spirit came upon me from the top of my head to the top of my shoulders, causing a great warmth and goosebumps! That moment gave me the assurance that I was already saved. I realized I was trying to become what I already was.

Those events were defining moments in my life when I figured out that the Spirit of God was coming upon me. My desire is to be able to help you communicate with the

Holy Spirit. This relationship with Him is a supernatural experience you can have when you learn to hear His voice.

Those who are of religion don't expect to hear the voice of our Father or the Holy Spirit because many denominations don't teach that He speaks to us in this day and time. When we understand the Kingdom, then we know we are the sons and daughters of our Heavenly Father (2 Corinthians 6:18). What father or parent does not talk to his children? What child does not want to talk with his or her parents? The Word says, "They who are led by the Spirit are the sons of God" (Romans 8:14). How can you fulfill your purpose on the earth if you don't know the voice of the Holy Spirit?

The Holy Spirit is a communicator. He wants to speak with us!

The Holy Spirit is a communicator. From the foundation of the world (Genesis) until now, He has wanted to communicate with man. He wants to speak with us! My goal is to help you to recognize His voice.

Sometimes He will speak through a man, a boy, a woman, or a girl. His voice won't always sound the same. It may be through your pastor, your parents, a friend, or a stranger. I have heard the voice of the Holy Spirit through my children. I have heard His voice speaking to my spirit in my own voice! I have also heard His voice as I read His Word. Sometimes when I listen to sermons or songs, I hear His voice within the message. You will begin to know when He is speaking to you. It will resonate in your spirit with an answer to a prayer. I know this may confound some of you, but by the time you finish reading this book, you will be able to recognize His voice.

To him the porter openeth; and the sheep hear his voice: and he calleth his own sheep by name, and leadeth them out.
And when he putteth forth his own sheep, he goeth before them, and the sheep follow him: for they know his voice. And a stranger will they not follow, but will flee from him: for they know not the voice of strangers. My sheep hear my voice, and I know them, and they follow me.

JOHN 10:3-5, 27

This is a very powerful statement Jesus made. Every born-again believer is a sheep, and that qualifies every believer to hear and recognize the voice of the Holy Spirit. **Read. That. Again.** Every born-again believer is a sheep, and that qualifies every believer to hear and recognize the voice of the Holy Spirit. What a blessing He has given us! When Jesus spoke to His disciples about the sheep recognizing the shepherd's voice, He meant the physical or tangible voice that is heard by human ears.

When Jesus released the Holy Spirit on the day of Pentecost, the Holy Spirit came and made His home in the spirits of men. To the best of my knowledge, there were only three people—John the Baptist, Elizabeth, and Zachariah—who received the Holy Spirit before the day of Pentecost (Luke 1:15).

I meet so many people who think God selects a certain few to whom He speaks. Who would want to have their father, son, or daughter never speak or communicate with them?

Even before we become sheep, the Holy Spirit begins to minister to us. The reason we surrender our lives to Him is because the Spirit of God is communicating with us so we will repent! Since He talks to us while we are yet sinners, think about how much more He wants to communicate with us after we accept Him. GOD CHOSE US FIRST! When we repent, we accept His calling.

But God commendeth his love toward us, in that,
while we were yet sinners, Christ died for us.

ROMANS 5:8

"No man can come to me, except the Father
which hath sent me draw him:
and I will raise him up at the last day.
It is written in the prophets,

And they shall be all taught of God
Every man therefore that hath heard,
and that learned of the Father, cometh unto me."

JOHN 6:44-45

"If ye then being evil, know how to give good gifts
unto your children: how much more shall
your heavenly Father give the Holy Spirit
to them that ask him?"

LUKE 11:13

Jesus is revealing Himself to us as a good Father. Since He gives us better gifts than we give our children, then surely He wants to talk to us also. I believe the Lord speaks to us daily in many different ways. I believe He talks to our spirits on a daily basis; we just fail to recognize that it is God speaking to us because we don't identify His voice.

Our Father spoke to His people many times throughout the Bible. The will of your heavenly Father is for you to know and recognize His voice. Throughout all of history, He has always communicated with man. He is NOT HIDING but steadily revealing Himself to those who hunger and thirst to know Him.

John 21:25 says that even the world itself could not contain all the books that could be written about all that Jesus did and all the words He spoke to man.

He is a good, good Father. He is not condemning us for our lack of knowledge or understanding. But He IS beckoning us to come sit at His feet and learn His voice. If we recognize His voice, then we can do what He desires for us to do. If we do NOT recognize His voice, we may never fulfill His purpose for our lives.

The first conversation recorded between man and God is with Adam in Genesis 2:16-17. We can conclude from Genesis 3:8, when both Adam and Eve identified that the voice they heard was the Lord's voice, that they must have spoken with Him beforehand.

If we recognize His voice, then we can do what He desires for us to do.

> *And they heard the voice of the Lord God*
> *walking in the garden in the cool of the day:*
> *and Adam and his wife hid themselves*
> *from the presence of the Lord God*
> *amongst the trees of the garden.*
>
> GENESIS 3:8

The following is a list of many occasions the Bible records when God spoke to man. Read each one and, in a few words, write down your thoughts to help you remember and reflect.

Adam and Eve in Genesis 2:16

_____

_____

Cain in Genesis 4:6

_____

_____

Noah in Genesis 6:13

_____

_____

Noah and his sons in Genesis 9:1

_____

_____

Abram in Genesis 12:1

_____

_____

Hagar in Genesis in 16:8

_____

_____

Sarai in Genesis 18:15

_____

_____

Rebekah in Genesis 25:23

_____

_____

Isaac in Genesis 26:2

_____

_____

Jacob in Genesis 28:13

_____

_____

Laban in Genesis 31:24

_____

_____

Pharaoh in Genesis 41:28

_____

_____

Israel in Genesis 46:2

_____

_____

Joseph in Genesis 47:5

_____

_____

Moses in Exodus 3:4

_____

_____

Aaron in Exodus 3:4

_____

_____

Balaam in Numbers 22:9

_____

_____

Joshua in Joshua 1:1

_____

_____

Samuel in 1 Samuel 3:4

_____

_____

David in 1 Samuel 23:2

_____

_____

Solomon in 1 Kings 3:5

_____

_____

Elijah in 1 Kings 19:9

_____

_____

Job in Job 38:1

_____

_____

Joseph in Matthew 1:20

_____

_____

Pilate's wife in Matthew 27:19

_____

_____

Thomas in John 20:27

_____

_____

The Apostles in Acts 5:20

_____

_____

Philip in Acts 8:26

_____

_____

Saul (Apostle Paul) in Acts 9:4

_____

_____

John in Revelation 1:10

_____

_____

The hearing ear, and the seeing eye,
the Lord hath made even both of them.

PROVERBS 20:12

The Hebrew word for hearing in this scripture verse is *shama*, and Strong's Concordance tells us it means to hear intelligently, attentively, to discern, to listen, to cause to hear, perceive, and understand.

The Hebrew word for seeing in this verse is *ra'ah*, which means to see (literally or figuratively), behold, discern, gaze, take heed, look, perceive, take sight of others, spy, stare, view, or have visions.

These words are both natural and spiritual. We know this because of what Jesus said: "Therefore speak I to them in parables: because they seeing see not; and hearing they hear not, neither do they understand" (Matthew 13:13-16).

God made us to be communicators and to hear Him. But religion (which is the traditions or doctrines of men) closes our eyes and our ears to the Kingdom (which is the truth AND our Father's way of doing things). Jesus rebuked the religious leaders of His day because they were standing in the way of people entering the truth of the Kingdom.

But woe to you, scribes and Pharisees, hypocrites!
For you shut up the kingdom of heaven against men;
for you neither go in yourselves,
nor do you allow those who are entering to go in.

MATTHEW 23:13 NKJV

The Kingdom is about developing a relationship with the Father, receiving Jesus Christ as your Lord and Savior, and being baptized in the Holy Spirit according to the book of Acts with the evidence of speaking in tongues. (You will learn more about this in another chapter.)

When we are in religion, which is man's way of reaching the Father, we can't see the Kingdom. Jesus and the supernatural are in the Kingdom. Everyone who is born again is born into the Kingdom of God. But religion prohibits you from understanding and walking in the Kingdom. The only way to walk in the Kingdom is to walk by faith.

For we walk by faith, not by sight.

2 CORINTHIANS 5:7 NKJV

Now the just shall live by faith: but if any man draw back, my soul shall have no pleasure in him.

HEBREWS 10:38

REFLECTION QUESTIONS
For Chapter 1

Have you ever wanted to hear the Father's voice?

_____

_____

_____

How did this chapter help you better understand how to go about hearing the Father's voice?

_____

_____

_____

What can you do RIGHT NOW to help you recognize that He is speaking to you?

_____

_____

_____

WORDS TO KNOW
Before Reading Chapter 2

Human Spirit—The inward man or spirit of man that lives for eternity

Baby Christian—A person who recently received Jesus into his or her heart and became born again spiritually or who has been a Christian for some time but has not yet grown in or gained knowledge of the Word of God

Gift of Prophecy—One of the nine spiritual gifts for all believers that speaks to another person or group of persons through inspiration by God for exhortation, edification, and comfort

2

Identifying the Voice of the Holy Spirit

I N GENESIS, GOD SPOKE everything into existence: every animal, plant, tree, dirt, stars, galaxies. But man, He built with His own hands. After He fashioned man, He looked upon him and saw he was without life. God bent over him and breathed air into his nostrils, and man became a living soul. This is the part of man that lives for eternity. The part of man that can never die. That is why we say at a gravesite, "From ashes to ashes and dust to dust." Man's body became the earth suit, the suitcase, the temple, not only for the human spirit but also for the Holy Spirit.

And what agreement hath the temple of God with idols? For ye are the temple of the living God; as God hath said, I will dwell in them, and walk in them; and I will be their God, and they shall be my people.
2 CORINTHIANS 6:16

The real part that lives for eternity is the part of man we can't see because he is a spirit as God is a Spirit. We are made in the image and likeness of God. God breathed into man, and when He did, man became a spirit being.

Now may the God of peace Himself sanctify you completely; and may your whole spirit, soul and body be preserved blameless at the coming of our Lord Jesus Christ.

1 THESSALONIANS 5:23 NKJV

Apostle Paul addressed man as a spirit first, then as a living soul and a body. Our spirit lives inside of us—the hidden or the inner man. We believe we are just mortal human beings, but the Word says we are immortal spirit beings. Our human body is just a shell for our spirit. James 2:26 AMP says, "For as the human body apart from the spirit is lifeless, so faith apart from [its] works of obedience is also dead." THIS IS VERY IMPORTANT TO REMEMBER.

God is a spirit, and He speaks to your spirit. Man is a living spirit living in an earth suit while on earth. God is living on the inside of what you see. For example, if you came to my condo on the ocean and I spoke to you through the door, you could hear me speaking to you, but you couldn't see me. That is the way man's spirit lives and operates within him. The Holy Spirit lives inside of our spirit. The Holy Spirit communicates with man's spirit. When He speaks to you, you must listen with your spirit and not with your ears. He is not speaking to your ears, but to your spirit. It is the Holy Spirit speaking to your spirit. His primary way of speaking to you is through your spirit which speaks to your mind.

We must learn how to still our mind and be able to distinguish the voice of the Holy Spirit from our own thoughts. He speaks so quietly. If you are not listening, you may not know He is speaking. Being able to listen for and actually hear the Holy Spirit speaking to you is a skill that must be developed.

Hearing the Lord speak to your spirit (learning to hear in your spirit what you don't hear in the natural and hearing with your inner man) must be developed or acquired. Being able to still the natural mind is a skill that is required in order to be tender and sensitive to hear the Holy Spirit. The more you learn His voice, the more softly He speaks. The more you know the Holy Spirit, the more tenderly He will speak to you because you can recognize His voice more clearly than in the beginning. This comes with experience. By hearing His voice over and over and over again, you become familiar with Him. The more you respond when He talks to you, the more He will talk to you.

A great example of NOT recognizing the voice of the Lord is in 1 Samuel. It is a challenge many people in the body of Christ have today.

And the child Samuel ministered unto the Lord before
Eli. And the word of the Lord was precious
in those days; there was no open vision.
And it came to pass at that time, when Eli was laid
down in his place, and his eyes began to wax dim,
that he could not see; And ere the lamp of God went
out in the temple of the Lord, where the ark of God
was, and Samuel was laid down to sleep;
That the Lord called Samuel:
and he answered, Here am I.
And he ran unto Eli, and said, Here am I;
for thou calledst me. And he said, I called not;
lie down again. And he went and lay down.
And the Lord called yet again, Samuel.
And Samuel arose and went to Eli,
and said, Here am I; for thou didst call me.
And he answered, I called not, my son; lie down again.
Now Samuel did not yet know the Lord,
neither was the word of the Lord
yet revealed unto him.
And the Lord called Samuel again the third time.
And he arose and went to Eli, and said,
Here am I; for thou didst call me.
And Eli perceived that the Lord had called the child.
Therefore Eli said unto Samuel, Go, lie down:
and it shall be, if he call thee, that thou shalt say,
Speak, Lord; for thy servant heareth.

So Samuel went and lay down in his place.
And the Lord came, and stood,
and called as at other times, Samuel, Samuel.
Then Samuel answered,
Speak; for thy servant heareth.

1 SAMUEL 3:1-10

Samuel was a child. When we are born again into the Kingdom of God, we come in as baby Christians, and we must learn to hear and recognize the voice of the Holy Spirit. When babies learn their parents' voices, though other people can be in the room speaking, when they hear their parents' voices, they always turn their heads toward the voice with

You must remember that the Father is not trying to hide His voice from you; nor is He trying to deceive you.

which they are familiar. They are familiar with those voices because they have spent time with them. Those familiar voices give them a feeling of comfort and love.

Becoming familiar with your Father's voice happens through repetition, spending time in the Word, in prayer, in praise and worship, and in meditation. You must remember that the Father is not trying to hide His voice from you; nor is He trying to deceive you.

Once you understand that He has a passion for you to know His voice, you will have more boldness and confidence in yourself to be able to hear Him. Remember, this is your Father speaking to His son or daughter.

Many people ask me how I know it is the Holy Spirit speaking to me. How do I know if it is another spirit? How do I know the difference? Remember, the number one way you learn to identify the Father's voice is by spending time with Him in His Word. If you hear a voice telling you to do something and you don't know who is speaking, remember this: If it is the Father or the Holy Spirit, what you hear will always come into alignment with the Bible, the Word of God. If it contradicts what the Bible says, then it is not the Holy Spirit, because He won't tell you something that does not line up with His Word.

When Samuel heard the voice of the Lord, he didn't recognize it, so he went to his pastor, Eli. When he went to Eli (a man of God), he asked if Eli had called out to him. Eli told Samuel that he had not called his name. Samuel went to Eli because when the Lord spoke to him, He sounded like Eli (his pastor or overseer).

Many times, when the Holy Spirit speaks to us, we don't recognize His voice because it sounds like our own voice. When we hear our spirit speaking to our mind, we don't consider it to be the Holy Spirit because it came through our voice. That is why after significant events happen, we sometimes say, "Something told me" or "It came to me" or "I had a prompting or a feeling, but I didn't know what to do with it." I pray this will lead you to a new understanding.

When the Holy Spirit (who dwells within us) speaks to our spirit, and our spirit speaks to our mind in our own voice, we often ask ourselves why that thought came to us. We feel certain it was not a normal thought for us; yet it was in our head. Why? Because the Holy Spirit often contradicts our innate common sense. Your senses tell you that what you heard makes no sense.

For example: You're sitting in a church service, and you had decided earlier you were going to give $25. Then something tells you to put $100 in the offering plate. You begin to wrestle with your common sense that you have only $25 in cash. Your mind further rationalizes that you need $75 to put gas in the car next week.

The carnal mind never tells you to do anything good for the body of Christ or for the Kingdom. But the Word tells you in Luke 6:38 to give and it will be given unto you. So, the Word confirms that what you heard is from the Holy Spirit.

Because the carnal mind is enmity against God:
for it is not subject to the law of God,
neither indeed can be.

ROMANS 8:7

When you are discerning about whether or not the voice you hear is from the Holy Spirit, remember this: Your carnal mind is an enemy to the Word of God. It is not saved. It works out of the natural realm. It always tries to make sense of everything. Many things which are spiritual don't make sense in the natural. The mind does not comprehend spiritual things. It thinks your thoughts are ridiculous or silly and don't make sense. But the things of God rarely make sense to your head.

I was sitting in a church service, and prior to the offering, the man of God asked us to pray about the amount to give. My mind was locked in on $25. The Holy Spirit spoke to me to give $500. I said "Satan, I bind you in the name of Jesus." Immediately, the Holy Spirit spoke to me and said, "Why would the enemy tell you to give to the Kingdom of God?" I had to repent for being fearful. I was afraid if I gave what He said, I wouldn't have enough to take care of my needs. That was the enemy trying to keep me from giving to the Kingdom to cut that ministry's blessings short and also to cut my blessings short. The Holy Spirit told me what to give. And that lined up with the Word of God. So, I gave the $500, knowing I would reap what I sowed.

The Holy Spirit always speaks to your inward man. Other voices must speak to your outward man. In the Old Testament, men didn't have the Spirit of God dwelling within them. So, when Samuel heard the voice of the

Lord calling him, he heard it with his natural ears (an audible voice). That is why he rose up and went to Eli to see what Eli wanted.

Sometimes when the Holy Spirit ministers to you, it sounds like the voice of someone who is a positive influence in your life. I have had several people tell me that the Lord spoke to them, and it sounded like my voice. Other people have said it sounded like my voice, their pastor's voice, or their teacher's voice. It can be anyone's voice with whom you are familiar.

If something does not line up with Scripture, it is not the Holy Spirit speaking.

Isn't it awesome that He can use a familiar voice with you because He wants to speak to you in a voice you will be comfortable with so you won't be afraid of what you are hearing? Remember, however, when you hear a familiar voice telling you something, it must still line up with the Word. If you hear a voice saying something that does not line up with Scripture, it is not the Holy Spirit speaking.

Let's return to the story of Eli. He realized the third time that Samuel was hearing from the Lord. So he gave him instructions and told him what he needed to do the next time the voice came to him. He told Samuel to say, "Speak, Lord, for your servant heareth."

There are so many people who think they have not heard the voice of the Holy Spirit. But once they are given instructions on how to identify His voice, they can hear Him speak to them clearly.

Samuel had not experienced hearing the Lord's voice before not only because he was young, but because the Lord was not speaking much in those days. So, he had not been taught to listen for Him. During that time, the Lord spoke through prophets. That is how Eli knew Samuel was a prophet. Eli asked Samuel what the Lord had said to him that night.

"Do you hear what these children are saying?" they asked him. "Yes," replied Jesus, "have you never read, 'From the lips of children and infants you, Lord, have called forth your praise'?"
MATTHEW 21:16 NIV

The high priest (Eli) sent a babe (Samuel) to hear what the Lord said. This is a good example to help us understand that age has nothing to do with your being available for God to speak to you and through you. Growth in our understanding of how to listen for the Holy Spirit's voice will help us in our daily walk with Him.

When we are inexperienced in knowing the voice of the Holy Spirit, sometimes we think God is working through calamities or is the cause of them. Elijah looked for the Lord when the wind broke the mountains, when the earthquake took place, and when the fire or lightning came down. But the Lord wasn't in those things.

And he said, Go forth, and stand upon the mount before the Lord. And, behold, the Lord passed by, and a great and strong wind rent the mountains, and brake in pieces the rocks before the Lord; but the Lord was not in the wind: and after the wind an earthquake; but the Lord was not in the earthquake: And after the earthquake a fire; but the Lord was not in the fire: and after the fire a still small voice. And it was so, when Elijah heard it, that he wrapped his face in his mantle, and went out, and stood in the entering in of the cave. And, behold, there came a voice unto him, and said, What doest thou here, Elijah?

1 KINGS 19:11-13

People often tend to blame God for earthquakes, hurricanes, floods, natural disasters. God does not want to kill what He died to save. This scripture shows that God was not in the broken rocks or the fire (destruction).

"The thief comes only to steal and kill and destroy; I (Jesus) came so that they would have life, and have it abundantly."

JOHN 10:10

Natural disasters kill, steal, and destroy. Why would Jesus have rebuked the storm (Mark 4: 35-41) if God orchestrated it?

So many times, we give credit to our enemy, the devil, for the negative complications that take place in our lives. What we don't realize is that the Father has already destroyed principalities. Because we are not aware of this, we self-destruct our own lives and destroy the lives of others around us because of our ignorance. The Father does not want us to be ignorant of His Word or of our authority. But Satan does! He wants to defeat us with our own ignorance. The Word tells us to choose life or death, blessing or cursing (Deuteronomy 30:19). When we choose death (anything contrary to God's Word) and it comes to pass, then we give the devil credit for it when he had nothing to do with it. Death comes to us because of our negative decisions.

"My people are destroyed for lack of knowledge: because thou hast rejected knowledge, I will also reject thee, that thou shalt be no priest to me; seeing thou hast forgotten the law of thy God, I will also forget thy children."

HOSEA 4:6

We often don't realize that our decisions not only affect us, they affect our children for generations to come. When I made the decision to leave North Carolina as a teenager to go to school in Kentucky and then to go to Indiana, it affected my unborn children and grandchildren. Because I chose to make a better life for myself, my now grown children and their children have a better life.

Because we don't have knowledge of or understand how the Holy Spirit moves, we hinder Him from speaking to us or through us. Once Samuel gave the Lord permission to speak, it changed his ministry forever! Eli was training Samuel in the physical works of ministry. But when the anointing came upon Samuel, the Spirit of the Lord trained him in the spiritual things.

The same thing is happening today—RIGHT NOW. You are being trained in one aspect of your life and ministry, and the Father wants to use this book as a tool to take you to the next dimension of spiritual knowledge.

I know this, by the Holy Spirit in me, that you are reading this book because you are hungry and thirsty for the deep concepts of the supernatural. He does not pour Himself out to just anyone or everyone but only to those who seek after Him. He said, "If you seek me, you shall find me."

"Ask, and it shall be given you; seek, and ye shall find; knock, and it shall be opened unto you: For everyone that asketh receiveth; and he that seeketh findeth; and to him that knocketh it shall be opened."

MATTHEW 7:7

He replied, "You are permitted to understand the secrets of the Kingdom of Heaven, but others are not."
MATTHEW 13:11 NLT

This is a word of knowledge for you that you will recognize His voice and be able to share with others what the Holy Spirit is saying to them. All you need is a desire and an understanding, and He will take care of the rest.

In the Old Testament, the Lord primarily spoke to believers through dreams, visions, visitations of angels, and sometimes even He Himself appeared to them. He had to speak to them through their five senses because Jesus had not yet been resurrected, nor had the Holy Spirit come to the earth to live and dwell in the spirits of men. The Holy Spirit could only *come upon* them in the Old Testament rather than *abide in* us as He does today.

Holy Spirit now speaks to our spirits. Romans 8:14 tells us, "They who are led by the Spirit (voice of the Holy Spirit) are the sons (spiritually mature) of God." He can trust you because you recognize His voice. You can't be led by the Holy Spirit or fulfill your purpose if you are unable to identify His voice guiding you.

You must train your mind to hear when God's Spirit is communicating to your spirit. It is very important to realize that God's desire is for you to recognize His voice because you are more than just a sheep. You are a son of the true Living God.

When you are a baby Christian, you should learn to recognize our Father's voice. You can sit a baby in a room with several adults and the baby may not pay anyone special attention. But when that baby hears a familiar voice, such as his parent's voice, you can see his body, ears, eyes, and actions respond to the familiar voice he has grown to recognize. He knows this familiar voice comforts him, feeds him, loves him, and embraces him when he is afraid or unsure.

And that which we don't see is more real than that which we do see.

This is the same way we should be toward our Father. We should be able to recognize His voice and feel comfortable with the things He has done for us. As we mature into sons, we become more conscious of what we don't hear with our natural ears and more conscious of that which is invisible rather than visible—what is *not* said more than what *is* said. And that which we *don't* see is more real than that which we *do* see. We can't see the Lord, but in Genesis, He spoke things out of the spirit into the natural. This tells us that natural, visible things are supported and produced by the invisible.

While we look not at the things which are seen, but at the things which are not seen:

for the things which are seen are temporal;
but the things which are not seen are eternal.

2 CORINTHIANS 4:18

For we walk by faith,
not by sight.

2 CORINTHIANS 5:7 NKJV

The Word of God calls us babes. When we become Christians, we are like babes feeding on the milk of the Word. We are supposed to be weaned from milk to bread. As we mature from being a child to an adult (sons of God), we begin to eat the meat of the Word. We all know that, to survive, babies must be fed with milk because they are not yet old enough to digest bread or meat. It would choke them. In the same way, as an infant grows from baby to toddler stage, he is able to eat bread and other soft foods. In the spiritual realm, we call this person "a child of God."

"Sons of God" are mature enough to exercise their spiritual as well as their natural senses.

In the same dimension, when the Word speaks about the "sons of God," it is referring to those who are mature enough to exercise their spiritual as well as their natural senses.

For though by this time you ought to be teachers,
you need someone to teach you again
the first principles of the oracles of God;
and you have come to need milk and not solid food.
For everyone who partakes only of milk
is unskilled in the word of righteousness,
for he is a babe. But solid food belongs to those
who are of full age, that is, those who by reason of use
have their senses exercised
to discern both good and evil.

HEBREWS 5:12-14 NKJV

One who recognizes the Holy Spirit when He is speaking to or through them is a mature person. As we mature, we recognize the voice of the Holy Spirit, and when He speaks to us about doing (or not doing) something, we will obey Him. We expect His presence to manifest in and through us in some form or fashion to help others. Some have a smile, a word of encouragement, a song, or a sermon that will bless others.

Well, my brothers and sisters, let's summarize.
When you meet together, one will sing, another will
teach, another will tell some special revelation God
has given, one will speak in tongues, and another will
interpret what is said. But everything that is done
must strengthen all of you.

1 CORINTHIANS 14:26 NLT

I believe, as we become mature sons in the things of the Lord, there is a demand on our life to do something or to minister to someone. A mature Christian looks outside of himself to see how to help others or to fulfill his call and the purpose that is upon his life. Baby Christians on milk or bread look inward, and their spiritual walk is about themselves: their sorrow, hurt, pain, shame, job, or marriage. Our spiritual walk should move us toward becoming a mature Christian who seeks to be a blessing to others.

The only way a man can communicate with the Father is by the spirit.

It is important for us to understand (as we become mature Christians) that man is made in the image and likeness of God. Because we are like our Father, then the things He desires, we desire. Every parent desires to communicate with their children. John 4:24 tells us that God is a Spirit, and those who worship Him must worship Him in spirit and in truth.

1 Thessalonians 5:23 tells us a man is a spirit, soul, and body. The only way a man can communicate with the Father is by the spirit. Because our Father desires us to communicate with Him, this should be our goal. Religion makes us afraid to say or to believe we can recognize our Father's voice. Religion wants us to call our Father *God*. But in 2 Corinthians 6:18, the Lord says if we come

out from unrighteousness and separate ourselves and touch not the unclean things, He will be a Father unto us, and we shall be His sons and His daughters.

It's in the Word that He adopted us as children through Jesus Christ (Ephesians 4:5, Galatians 1:5, Romans 8:23). When we understand that Father is looking for a family, then we have no need to walk around and call Him *God*, but rather we should call Him *Father*. That is His honorable and respectful place in our lives.

I have said all of that to bring you to this place. Father wants you to recognize His voice. The enemy does not want you to believe this is possible. An old hymn says, "He walks with me, and He talks with me, and He tells me I am His own." So, the whole purpose of this book comes down to the next few paragraphs. I want to make it clear to you that you CAN hear and DO hear Father's voice. I just need to help you by the grace of the Holy Spirit.

The Father has been speaking all the time. You just didn't recognize His voice. Let me give you some examples of how I hear His voice. Many people say I am a prophet. Some say I am an apostle or an evangelist, and many people call me pastor. I would like to think of myself as a teacher. But I realize I am not, after hearing my pastor and my pastor's pastor. I know that I am a long way from being a teacher. I want you to understand that a title is not necessary to be able to hear His voice. What

IS necessary is to be born again. Even before you became born again, Father talked to you. You just didn't recognize His voice. Jesus said in John 6:44, "No man can come to Me, except the Father which hath sent me draw him." So, before we were even washed in the blood of the Lamb, Father was talking to us. He was talking to you because He already called you. He already chose you from the foundation of the world (John 15:16).

I want to give you some everyday practical common sense ways to hear God's voice. Donis (my wife) asked me one day to teach her how to hear God's voice like I do. That was a challenge for me at that time because I didn't yet know how to tell her that God's voice sounds like your own voice because God (the Holy Spirit) lives inside of you in your spirit.

> *The Holy Spirit will usually answer us in our own voice.*

When we ask the Holy Spirit, He will usually answer us in our own voice. When we are not listening or focused, then He will use another method or way to communicate with us because we have become so familiar with our voice. He communicates to our spirit, and our spirit communicates it to our brain.

When the voice of the Lord comes to me through others, He is using their external or outward voice to speak to me in a way that bears witness to my spirit. I recognize that it is the word of the Lord coming to me through that person.

The next few pages will bring this into focus. I declare it is made plain unto you what I am about to say. John 14:26 says the Holy Spirit Himself is the teacher. That Great Teacher lives within you.

When my wife asked me this, I asked the Holy Spirit how to teach her. I paused and waited for Him to say something. He said to tell her He would speak to her during the offering time. Let me explain. When we go to church, we always ask the Holy Spirit what to put in the offering, and He always tells me what to put in. Sometimes the amount He tells me to give is comfortable, and sometimes it hurts. But I obey because He is telling me.

So, when we went to church that Sunday morning, I asked the Holy Spirit what to put in the offering and I asked Him to tell Donis what to put in the offering. She asked me how she would know if it was the Holy Spirit or not. I told her not to listen with her head. She said, "I don't understand." I told her, "Just ask and then be still, and He will tell you."

She took about thirty seconds and looked at me and said, "He told me $50." I smiled and said, "You're right!" She told me it sounded as if she were talking to herself. I told her that was her spirit speaking to her.

Remember, the Holy Spirit talks to your spirit, and your spirit talks to you. I often share with people that the

Lord always tells you to do things you wouldn't ordinarily do. Whatever the Lord tells you to do ALWAYS comes in line with His Word. Once you learn the Word, you begin to learn God's character. His character is always consistent with His Word. Once you know a person, when someone says something negative about them, you can say you know that is not their character because you know them. We need to be in the Word and get to know our Father.

If I were to tell you I'd rather go to an ice hockey game than have a chicken dinner, you would say, "That's not Brother Johnnie." But if I would tell you I love to have chicken every day and if you wanted to fix it, that would be fine, you would say, "Now THAT'S Brother Johnnie!" That sounds more like what I would want.

The Word tells us that the thief comes to steal, kill, and destroy. So, if what you're hearing doesn't line up with "life and life more abundantly," then you know you're not hearing the Holy Spirit. We don't listen to hear Father's voice with our external ear; we listen to hear His voice with our internal ear. He always speaks to us from within because He resides in our "belly," the center of our being. This is how and why you listen with your "inner" ear! If you are going to be a mouthpiece for the Lord, you must master identifying His voice.

Another time my wife and I were working on recognizing His voice, we were in a church service and the gentleman receiving the offering asked us to pray about what to give. I didn't feel the power of the Holy Spirit flowing through him. My head said to give him $25. But I asked the Holy Spirit, and He blew me out of the water when He said to give the man $500! I said, "Lord, if this is You, please tell Donis the same thing." Then I asked her to ask the Lord how much to put in. About ten to fifteen seconds later, I knew He told her the same amount because it took her a long time to respond. She looked up with one eye open and answered, "He said a whole lot!" I said, "I know! He said a whole lot to me, too. Hurry up because the offering basket is coming." I elbowed her and asked her how much. She said, "$500." I told her, "That's what I got too." So, we sowed that into this man's ministry.

I told the Lord I needed money to pay my taxes. I owed $1,800 for both state and federal, so it was hard to understand why we were told to give $500 to the offering. I was twenty-three years old at the time. We had $873 in our checking account. Our friends (who had come with us to the service) asked if they could borrow $300 until they got home. We gave it to them for their offering. The offering was received at 8:30 p.m.

When I got home, there was a message on my answering machine from my accountant. It had come in at exactly 8:30 p.m. She asked me to come to her office the next day. When we arrived, she told us that as she was eating dinner the previous night, it came to her that she should go back five years on our taxes to get more money back. I said, "Amen and thank you, Jesus!" It changed from us owing $1,800 to us receiving $4,800 and some change that year. We listened to the voice of the Lord, obeyed the voice of the Lord, and reaped immediately from our obedience. So, you can see there are great benefits to hearing and obeying what the Lord asks us to do.

The enemy is the one who brings fear and tells us we can't recognize our Father's voice and that we are not worthy to share the Good News with others. He will always tell you what you can't do. He will always bring you to a halt. You must remember he is a thief and a liar. Jesus said the enemy has been around from the very beginning, from the foundation of time. Faith (the opposite of fear) always needs action—moving, doing, and being—if you are going to flow in the supernatural.

Faith always needs action if you are going to flow in the supernatural.

As a teenager, I would try to hear the voice of the Father by "fleecing" Him instead of learning His voice. I used to pray and ask Him questions such as, "If this be Your will let there be one blackbird on the clothesline. Or if the answer is no, then let there be two birds." I got confused when there were no birds. I didn't know what the Father wanted me to do. I believe that was the first step in having a more passionate desire to hear His voice.

I used to lie in the cornfield at night after harvest. I would look up at the stars or the moon and ask Father to speak to me. I still remember my mother coming to the door and asking me if I was okay. She could hear me crying out to the Lord. I was afraid I was going to be just another ordinary Christian. I had a desire for the supernatural. I had a desire to know Father. The first step in being able to recognize Father's voice is to have a strong desire, a passion and zeal for the supernatural.

Father never just gives Himself away. The Word says if we pursue Him, He will pursue us. In my younger days, I desired to prophesy more than I desired to eat. And, believe me, I did love to eat! I could eat a chicken and all the trimmings and still have room for dessert. Thank God for deliverance!

One Thursday afternoon when I was at Job Corps, Fred, a minister friend of mine, asked me what I desired to do for the Lord. I told him I desired to prophesy. We always had church on Saturday at noon. We all came to the altar for different reasons. When Fred got to me, he laid hands on me and said to me, "The Lord has released on you the spirit of prophecy. Go ahead and start prophesying even now!" I said to myself, "He is only saying that because he asked me that question on Thursday. I am not going to play with the Lord and just say something because Fred told me to." So, I just stood there and said, "Thank you, Jesus!" because I didn't want to misrepresent the Holy Spirit.

So as days and weeks went on, Holy Spirit's voice became clearer to me. We used to go to a Full Gospel church called the Sheep Shed in Corydon, Kentucky. After the praise and worship, there was always a time we would pause to give the Holy Spirit an opportunity to speak. One Friday night, I heard the Holy Spirit speak to me. He was giving me a word for the congregation. I got nervous and froze. The devil said to me "What if this is only you?" So, I said to the Holy Spirit, "If this be You, give someone else the same words You've given me so the next time I will know the words were from You. I just want to be sure I don't say something You're not saying." Someone gave the same four words I had received, and I was so excited I could have run around the building several times because I realized I now recognized Father's voice.

The next week in service the same routine took place. I got nervous again and said, "Lord, if this be You, let someone else say it so I can be sure." Once again, someone gave the same words I had. I was so excited that I began to tell my friends and the people in the congregation that I could hear His voice! They just gave me a religious look like "sure you can," "oh yeah," "that's good."

They patted me on the back and gave me a religious smile before they walked off. But I wanted to do a jig! This was a lifelong dream come true for me.

The fifth time I received a word from the Father, I opened my mouth and began to speak. I had only three or four words, so I was not sure what I was going to say beyond the fourth word, but once I started to speak, I heard the Father say other things.

You don't have to hear it all before saying it. Sometimes you just hear a few words, and then as you speak, more will come. I have learned to listen and go with the flow. I used to give a word to the whole body of Christ (the church), and it took about five to six seconds. Now it takes me about five or six minutes to give a word to one person. I didn't start out prophesying to just one person, because you have to be able to hear clearly when you speak to an individual rather than to a whole body. Then I started seeing pictures in my mind to share with people. The Lord used to give me a mental picture, and I would describe the picture I saw to that person. Somehow, someway, when I shared the picture, they knew it was from the Lord.

For years, I had pictures in my mind when I prophesied to a person one on one. I had to touch the person in order to have a clear word. Now, I can prophesy to people without touching them and even prophesy by phone with accuracy.

There have been times when I was on my television program that I got a word of knowledge from the Lord for someone. I described the situation someone was in and then told them what to do or what the Lord said He was going to do.

I used to have to be in a church or religious setting in order to have a word, but now I can be standing in line at a restaurant and anticipate the nudging of the Holy Spirit to minister to the cashier or the person in front of or behind me. Sometimes they are believers and sometimes they are not. Some of them are from other religious denominations, but they almost always acknowledge that what I said to them was true and accurate. They often ask how I knew or if I knew any of their friends or family. I tell them the Holy Spirit told me.

What you say may not sound very spiritual to you, but to the person receiving, it is life changing.

What you say may not sound very spiritual to you, but to the person receiving, it is life changing. The Word says not to despise a small beginning (Zechariah 4:10). So take baby steps, and the Father will add to you. Be faithful in little, and the Holy Spirit will give you much. You work your way up by exercising the gift. For practice, you can prophesy to your friends, family, or church associates, and ask them if what you're saying bears witness with them. This helps you know if you're hearing from the Lord. We all develop by practice.

To hear from the Holy Spirit and know the heart of the Father, it's important to have an attitude of true humility and service. We can see by the following that it doesn't always come naturally.

Then the mother of Zebedee's sons came to Jesus
with her sons and, kneeling down,
asked a favor of him.
"What is it you want?" he asked.
She said, "Grant that one of these two sons of mine
may sit at your right and the other at your left
in your kingdom."
"You don't know what you are asking,"
Jesus said to them.
"Can you drink the cup I am going to drink?"
"We can," they answered.
Jesus said to them, "You will indeed
drink from my cup, but to sit at my right or left
is not for me to grant.
These places belong to those for whom
they have been prepared by my Father."
When the ten heard about this,
they were indignant with the two brothers. Jesus
called them together and said, "You know that the

rulers of the Gentiles lord it over them, and their high officials exercise authority over them. Not so with you. Instead, whoever wants to become great among you must be your servant, and whoever wants to be first must be your slave—just as the Son of Man did not come to be served, but to serve, and to give his life as a ransom for many."

MATTHEW 20:20-28

If anyone should be served, it should be Jesus. But he came to be our example. To serve whom? The poor, the rejected, the middle class, upper class, the rich. Whoever needs us. Those are the ones we are to serve.

You don't prophesy because you want respect; you prophesy because you are called to serve people.

You don't prophesy because you want respect; you prophesy because you are called to serve people. You can recognize those prophets who are out for themselves because they won't sacrifice to serve. They have excuses.

Jesus told James and John that the greater you are, the more you will suffer. Can you bear this bitterness or take this pressure? Look how great Paul was, and then look at all he suffered. To a servant, the suffering is worth it. The Father is the one who predestined us.

If I have done this,
you should do the same thing I have done.

JOHN 13:15

For to this you were called,
because Christ also suffered for us,
leaving us an example,
that you should follow His steps.

1 PETER 2:21

Reflection Questions
for Chapter 2

The Holy Spirit speaks to you through your heart or your spirit. What are some ways you can prepare to be able to hear the Holy Spirit talking to you?

_____

_____

_____

How can you be sure that what you hear from the Holy Spirit is actually from the Holy Spirit?

_____

_____

_____

How can you become better at hearing the Holy Spirit speak to you?

_____

_____

_____

When the Holy Spirit speaks to you, what should you do with what He tells you?

_____

_____

_____

Why is it important to have a servant's heart when you prophesy?

_____

_____

_____

Words to Know
Before Reading Chapter 3

Patriarch—The father and ruler of a family, tribe, or race in biblical history; a title commonly applied to Abraham, Isaac, and Jacob

Exhort—To encourage, inspire, or build a person up

Dominion—The power or right to govern and control

Kingdom Authority—Having dominion given by God along with the ability or power to carry out that assignment

3

Why the Holy Spirit Speaks to You

KNOWING WHY FATHER wants to speak to us helps us want to converse with Him. If He spoke to His patriarchs Abraham, Moses, Isaac, Jacob, and Joseph, and they were servants of God, how much more will He talk to His own sons and daughters?

First and most important, Father wants to speak to us (and wants us to hear Him) because He wants us to know how much He loves us.

Religion and/or the devil want us to see our heavenly Father as an angry God. When catastrophes such as hurricanes, tornadoes, earthquakes, and other natural disasters occur, people call them *acts of God*. Jesus said the enemy comes to steal, kill, and destroy (John 10:10). Jesus came that we may have life and have it abundantly. It is the enemy who destroys, and if these things are of the enemy, then we have authority over them.

Jesus spoke to the storm and commanded it to cease, and it obeyed (Mark 4:39). And He said, "He who believes in me will also do the works that I do; and greater works than these will he do" (John 14:12).

In Genesis 1:26, God said He gave man dominion over the earth. In Ephesians 1:22, He said that Christ is the head of the church, and He has put all things under His feet. Jesus is the head of the body. We are the body, and all things are under our feet. That means we have dominion and power over the enemy.

"Behold I give unto you power to tread on serpents and scorpions, and over all the power of the enemy: and nothing shall by any means hurt you."

LUKE 10:19

We must exert that power and authority to thwart the enemy's plans. It is given to us to take control over our situations and problems. Mark 11:23 tells us to speak to our mountains and they shall obey us.

As they say in the Carolinas, God works in mysterious ways. That is why people, in general, see our heavenly Father as mean and angry. They hesitate to pray to Him, because they believe they are not good enough to come to Him. They believe if Father has anything to say, it will be a punishment for many different things: not going to church on Sunday, wearing inappropriate clothing, or breaking any other "rule."

Because we see Father as angry, we fail to believe that He wants to communicate with us—or, if He does, it's because we've done something wrong, and He wants to let us know He's angry. Our Father is not angry at us. That kind of thinking is the result of wrong doctrines and the traditions of men that have distorted our beliefs.

Many are focused on the law rather than on their relationship with the Father. For example, they believe if an unwed woman becomes pregnant, it is punishment for having sex outside of marriage, when it is simply the principle of sowing and reaping. If a person falls out of a tree and gets hurt, they believe it is punishment for being disobedient. Actually, it is just the law of gravity.

Because we see Father as angry, we fail to believe that He wants to communicate with us.

There are natural consequences that don't have anything to do with the Father or the devil, yet people blame the Father. Job's friends blamed his sin for the things that happened to him and his family. All of these things cause people to not want to communicate with the Father because they are afraid He is angry or displeased with them.

Too often, we stand around and wait on our heavenly Father to do something to fix our circumstances or situations, and when nothing positive takes place, we go down in defeat. Then, the next time a similar challenge or circumstance comes up, we remember the last failure. We chicken out on faith because it didn't work the last time, when the reality is, as Hosea 4:6 says, God's people are destroyed for the lack of knowledge.

In Mark 11:13, Jesus said the tradition of men causes the Word to have no effect. We wait on Father to work something out on our behalf, and He doesn't show up. Why? Because He is the God of the impossible, not the God of the possible. Many times, we wait for our prayers to be answered, but those answers don't manifest because we have not done our part. The Holy Spirit will never do for us what we can do for ourselves. He has given man dominion and authority in the earth. Always remember, the Holy Spirit will only do the impossible if you have done everything you think is possible.

At times, I come across believers who say they are waiting on Father to fix this or change that, and it is something they can do for themselves. Then, when Father does not move on their behalf, they say that faith does not work.

Our circumstances have nothing to do with faith. We struggle because of our lack of knowledge. Then, the enemy tells us that our faith is not working, and that brings us shame, doubt, unbelief, and being hesitant to trust God the next time. Down the road, we are destroyed because we have the wrong concept of our Father. If you are in a situation in which there is nothing you can do or you have no knowledge of what to do, then Father can and will intervene on your behalf. But we must give Father something to work with. This is very, very important for us to understand. Father will only intervene on your behalf when you can't do it for yourself. We must first do all that we can do, and then He will do what we can't do.

When I talk about having a personal relationship with the Father, I encounter people who say they aren't a preacher or a prophet, a missionary, or anything that would be considered important. You are very important because Jesus made the ultimate sacrifice for you. You don't give your life for someone who is worthless. You only give your life (or make a sacrifice) for someone you value immensely.

We hear the old cliché of John 3:16 all the time, but how many times do we stop and really take a look at what the Lord is saying to us?

For God so loved the world, that He gave His only begotten Son, that whosoever believeth in Him should not perish, but have everlasting life.

JOHN 3:16

The Lord is telling you He sacrificed the best He had for you. So, if He sacrificed the best offering He could give—the life of His only begotten Son—then He wants to communicate with you. You are not only someone worthwhile, you are a son or a daughter of God Himself.

And I will be a Father unto you, and ye shall be My sons and My daughters, saith the Lord Almighty.

2 CORINTHIANS 6:18

How can it be that the God of the universe wants us to call Him *Daddy*?

*According as he hath chosen us in him
before the foundation of the world,
that we should be holy and without blame
before him in love:
Having predestinated us unto the adoption of children
by Jesus Christ to himself,
according to the good pleasure of his will.*

EPHESIANS 1:4-5

If He is our Daddy, then He wants to love us, communicate with us, and help us in any situation in which we find ourselves. Religion teaches us to communicate with our Father only when there is trouble. I often hear people say, "My children call me, not because they are interested in me or care about my situation, but only when they want or need something." Many times, we as God's sons and daughters have that same mentality. We only talk to Dad when we need something.

But He wants to hear from us daily, and not only to hear about our challenges or troubles. He tells us to speak to the mountain about Him rather than talk to Him about the mountain.

He wants us to praise Him and worship Him. He wants to hear how awesome a Father He is. He desires us to thank and exhort Him and seek after Him.

Seek the Lord while He may be found;
call on Him while He is near.

ISAIAH 55:6 NIV

And you will seek Me and find Me,
when you search for Me with all your heart.

JEREMIAH 29:13

God did this so that they would seek him
and perhaps reach out for him and find him,
though he is not far from any one of us.

ACTS 17:27 NIV

When I am counseling or consulting, I often discover that people believe if they fast or pray hard enough, the Holy Spirit will communicate with them. The Holy Spirit wants to talk with us more than we want to talk with Him. He has so many things He wants to reveal to us about our family, ministry, health, finances, and every-day situations. He already knows and wants to share with us if we will give Him permission. We often say with words that we give Him permission, but we don't expect or believe He wants to talk with us. We don't listen. This is a part of culture, religion, and traditions. Remember that Jesus said the traditions of men cause the Holy Spirit not to speak (cause the Word to have no effect).

Take a moment and think about your own children. What do you want them to do for you and to you? How do you want them to love and respect you? Our heavenly Father deeply desires that same kind of love and respect. Remember, we are made in the likeness and image of our heavenly Father (Genesis 1:26). He wants to converse with us simply because He made us and loves us.

Father has some things He wants to say to you personally. He wants to speak with you directly.

Father has some things He wants to say to you personally that He does not want to tell you through another person. He wants to speak with you directly. He wants you to know His will, His way, and to have the confidence that when you need your Father, He is there for you. Remember, His mercy endures for a thousand generations. He loves you with all of His life.

Romans 8:32 tells us, "He that spared not his own Son, but delivered him up for us all, how shall he not with him also freely give us all things?" He said He will freely give you all things.

For when we were yet without strength,
in due time Christ died for the ungodly.

ROMANS 5:6

If Christ died for the ungodly, what will He do for the godly?

For scarcely for a righteous man will one die:
yet peradventure for a good man
some would even dare to die.
But God commendeth his love toward us,
in that, while we were yet sinners,
Christ died for us.

ROMANS 5:7-8

God didn't ask us if we wanted Him to love us; He just loved us. Even while we were yet His enemies, He still loved us.

Much more then, being now justified by His blood,
we shall be saved from wrath through Him.

ROMANS 5:9

Because we have been justified, the wrath of God is not going to come upon us.

For if, when we were enemies, we were reconciled to
God by the death of his Son, much more, being
reconciled, we shall be saved by his life.

ROMANS 5:10

This tells us that God has our backs. When we weren't even a son or a daughter, this is what He did for us. How much more will He do for us now?

And all things are of God,
who hath reconciled us to himself by Jesus Christ,
and hath given to us the ministry of reconciliation;
To wit, that God was in Christ,
reconciling the world unto himself,
not imputing their trespasses unto them;
and hath committed unto us
the word of reconciliation.

2 CORINTHIANS 5:18-19

God didn't wait until we were cleaned up. He embraced us while we were in the pigpen, while we were in the midst of doing unholy things and being in unholy places. He came with Jesus to get us and bring us back to Him. He told the devil, "I am not going to let you have My kids. I am going to defeat you and crush your head. I, Myself, am coming after My kids." God didn't send Gabriel or the angels; He showed up Himself.

We have to get rid of the religious mindset and its false beliefs that tell us we are not good enough. We have been embracing the lie that we are unworthy and thinking it is the truth because of hurts we have suffered and thinking those sufferings were God's will.

So we are Christ's ambassadors,
God making His appeal as it were through us.
We [as Christ's personal representatives] beg you for
His sake to lay hold of the divine favor [now offered
you] and be reconciled to God.

2 CORINTHIANS 5:20 AMPC

We are personal ambassadors for God. We have favor with God. We need to read that Word daily to remind us who we are and what we are. God is not *going to do*; He *already has done.*

His divine power has given to us all things
that pertain to life and godliness,
through the knowledge of Him
who called us by glory and virtue.

2 PETER 1:3 NKJV

It is important for us to know that our Father is for us and not against us.

What shall we then say to these things?
If God be for us, who can be against us?

He that spared not his own son, but delivered him up
for us all, how shall he not with him
also freely give us all things?

ROMANS 8:31-32

Beloved, let us love one another:
for love is of God; and every one that loveth
is born of God, and knoweth God.
He that loveth not knoweth not God; for God is love.

1 JOHN 4:7-8

Often, we see Father as the God of the universe, too big to be touched with our natural human minds. But He doesn't want to be just God in our personal relationship; He wants to be our Father.

He wants us to not be just His sheep or servants; He wants us to be His sons and daughters. He wants to have an intimate and personal relationship with us.

And what agreement hath the temple of God
with idols? For ye are the temple of the living God;
as God hath said,
I will dwell in them, and walk in them;
and I will be their God,
and they shall be my people.

2 CORINTHIANS 6:16

I will be a Father to you,
And you shall be My sons and daughters,
says the Lord Almighty.

2 Corinthians 6:18 NKJV

"Henceforth I call you not servants;
for the servant knoweth not what His Lord doeth:
but I have called you friends;
for all things that I have heard of my Father
I have made known unto you."

John 15:15

Ye are of God, little children,
and have overcome them:
because greater is he that is in you,
than he that is in the world.

1 John 4:4

Another reason the Holy Spirit wants to speak to us is to teach us and bring all things to our remembrance. The job of the Holy Spirit is to remind us of what the Father has already promised us. He must be able to talk to us, and we must be able to hear Him. Most people don't take time to think about this. We know He is the teacher, and in order for Him to teach, we must be able to hear.

Anyone with ears to hear must listen to the Spirit
and understand what he is saying.

Revelation 2:29 NLT

It is the Holy Spirit who brings us revelation, enlightenment, and understanding of Scripture so we can apply the Word and the gifts of the Holy Spirit to our life.

I want you to know, brothers and sisters, that the gospel I preached is not of human origin. I did not receive it from any man, nor was I taught it; rather, I received it by revelation from Jesus Christ.
GALATIANS 1:11-12 NIV

The key is having an ear to hear the Holy Spirit. Everyone has ears, but not everyone has ears to listen to or be aware of what the Holy Spirit is saying. The Lord was talking to Samuel and calling him by name even when Samuel didn't yet know the Lord and the Word of the Lord had not yet been revealed to him (1 Samuel 3:7). He does the same with us. He calls us.

Everyone has ears, but not everyone has ears to listen to or be aware of what the Holy Spirit is saying.

He saved us and called us with a holy calling, not according to our own accomplishments, but according to his own purpose and the grace that was given to us in the Messiah Jesus before time began.
2 TIMOTHY 1:9 ISV

The Word must be revealed to us by the Holy Spirit.

But the Comforter, which is the Holy Ghost, whom the Father will send in my name, he shall teach you all things, and bring all things to your remembrance, whatsoever I have said unto you.

JOHN 14:26

Since the Holy Spirit is the teacher, how can He teach us without speaking to us? This should give us confidence to know that He has a desire to communicate with us daily. He desires to give us revelation knowledge about everyday issues through the reading and meditation of the Word and praying in the Spirit (tongues) as in Romans 8:26-27. Your spirit searches the Holy Spirit within you in order to know the Lord's perfect will and purpose for your life. This can't manifest unless you have your prayer language, which you will read about soon.

Our ability to hear the Holy Spirit speak to us and our ability to communicate with Him help us understand our God-given purpose and how we should go about fulfilling it.

In Acts 9, the Lord told the prophet Ananias that Paul was called to the Gentiles. Paul knew his purpose through a word from the Lord. Many people don't know their purpose because they are not aware of the Holy Spirit's voice. The Holy Spirit revealed Paul's purpose to him.

The Holy Spirit is our guide, counselor, and teacher. Jesus said this:

"But the Comforter, which is the Holy Ghost, whom the Father will send in My name, He shall teach you all things, and bring all things to your remembrance, whatsoever I have said unto you."

JOHN 14:26

The Amplified version explains it this way:

But the Comforter (Counselor, Helper, Intercessor, Advocate, Strengthener, Standby), the Holy Spirit, Whom the Father will send in My name [in My place, to represent Me and act on My behalf], He will teach you all things. And He will cause you to recall (will remind you of, bring to your remembrance) everything I have told you.

JOHN 14:26 AMPC

Here are the definitions of the words the Amplified Bible uses to describe who the Comforter is:

Counselor—A person who gives advice or counseling

Helper—One who helps

Intercessor—One who intercedes in prayer, petition, or entreaty in favor of or on behalf of another

Advocate—One who pleads the cause of another; one who defends or maintains a cause or proposal; one who supports or promotes the interests of another

Strengthener—One who makes stronger or helps someone to become stronger

Standby—One to be relied on, especially in emergencies; a favorite or reliable choice or resource; one who is held in reserve ready for use

You can see that the Holy Spirit does not speak to us to condemn or to punish us but to comfort and help us. For Him to do those things for us, we must be able to connect with Him.

There is therefore now no condemnation
to them which are in Christ Jesus,
who walk not after the flesh, but after the Spirit.

ROMANS 8:1

The Holy Spirit does and will convict us when we have done wrong so we can correct ourselves. There are consequences of our actions, but the Holy Spirit does not condemn us or pass judgment on us. Jesus didn't judge or condemn the woman who was caught in the act of adultery.

So when they continued asking him, he lifted up himself, and said unto them, He that is without sin among you, let him first cast a stone at her.

JOHN 8:7

Saul, whose name God changed to Paul, asked the Lord what He wanted, and the Lord spoke to him and then sent Ananias to him to lay hands on him and tell him all the things he must suffer.

And Saul, yet breathing out threatenings and slaughter against the disciples of the Lord, went unto the high priest, And desired of him letters to Damascus to the synagogues, that if he found any of this way, whether they were men or women, he might bring them bound unto Jerusalem. And as he journeyed, he came near Damascus: and suddenly there shined round about him a light from heaven: And he fell to the earth, and heard a voice saying unto him, Saul, Saul, why persecutest thou me? And he said Who art thou, Lord? And the Lord said, I am Jesus whom thou persecutest: it is hard for thee to kick against the pricks. And he trembling and astonished said, Lord, what wilt thou have me to do? And the Lord said unto him Arise and go into the city, and it shall be told thee what thou must do.

ACTS 9:1-6

It took two people, Saul and Ananias, to recognize the voice of the Holy Spirit for Saul to know his purpose.

There are many examples in Scripture where the Lord spoke to His people to give them instruction and direction for their survival and purpose. Elijah was one of the greatest prophets who ever lived. We can see the importance of being able to recognize the voice of the Holy Spirit when the Lord spoke to Elijah and gave him personal instructions about where to go to survive the drought.

And Elijah the Tishbite, who was of the inhabitants of Gilead, said unto Ahab, As the Lord God of Israel liveth, before whom I stand, there shall not be dew nor rain these years, but according to my word.
And the word of the Lord came unto him, saying, Get thee hence, and turn thee eastward, and hide thyself by the brook Cherith, that is before Jordan.
And it shall be, that thou shalt drink of the brook; and I have commanded the ravens to feed thee there.

1 KINGS 17: 1-4

The Lord instructed Noah to build something that had never been built. There had never been a reason to build an ark because it had never rained before. Because Noah recognized the voice of the Lord and knew he could trust Him, he was able to save his own life and that of his entire family.

And God said unto Noah,
The end of all flesh is come before me;
for the earth is filled with violence through them;
and, behold, I will destroy them with the earth.
Make thee an ark of gopher wood ...

GENESIS 6:13-14

Here are more examples in which the Lord spoke to men about becoming missionaries:

Now the word of the Lord came unto Jonah
the son of Amittai, saying, Arise, go to Nineveh,
that great city, and cry against it;
for their wickedness is come up before me.

JONAH 1:1-2

And the angel of the Lord spake unto Philip,
saying, Arise, and go toward the south
unto the way that goeth down
from Jerusalem unto Gaza, which is desert.

ACTS 8:26

Philip was led to catch up with a chariot to talk to a eunuch who served the Candace or Queen of Ethiopia. Philip preached to him, and the man believed him and was water baptized. If Philip had not heard and obeyed the Lord, the eunuch would not have received Christ as His Lord and Savior. It is said by the Abyssinians of

Ethiopia that the queen took the Gospel back to her country, which came to know Jesus Christ because Philip heard and obeyed the Holy Spirit. The ability to hear God's word puts you in a position to bring God's will to pass. God speaks to man to reveal the Holy Spirit's purpose to us and instruct us away from our own purposes. The Holy Spirit led Peter away from his prejudice because he didn't believe that anyone could be born again unless they were a Jew. So, the Lord showed him a vision and spoke to him to go with the men who were at the door seeking him. The Lord directed Peter from his will to the Lord's will (Acts 10:9-11, 19-20).

On the morrow, as they went on their journey, and drew nigh unto the city Peter went up upon the housetop to pray about the sixth hour: And he became very hungry, and would have eaten: but while they made ready, he fell into a trance, and saw heaven opened. ... While Peter thought on the vision, the Spirit said unto him, Behold, three men seek thee. Arise therefore, and get thee down, and go with them, doubting nothing: for I have sent them.

This is a good example of how important it is to be able to recognize the voice of the Holy Spirit, because Cornelius's family and about one hundred soldiers gave their lives to the Lord because of Peter's ability to recognize the voice of the Holy Spirit.

Arise, go to Zarephath, which belongs to Sidon,
and dwell there. Behold, I have commanded
a widow there to provide for you.

1 KINGS 17:9

This is a great example of the widow woman who heard both the voice of the Lord and Elijah's voice. If she had not listened and obeyed, she and her son would have perished. Because she heard and obeyed, not only did she and her son survive, but Elijah the prophet also lived.

It was equally important for Elijah to hear and obey. He had to leave a place where the Lord had provided for him to go to Zarephath. He was leaving the familiar. Too often we fail to understand that what the Holy Spirit is saying to us is only for a season. If Elijah had not recognized this, he would have died at the brook.

Abraham experienced this also when he was told to sacrifice his son. As he was bringing down the blade, the angel of the Lord spoke to him to do Isaac no harm. It is crucial for believers to have a "now word" from the Holy Spirit in order to follow His will daily.

A now word is the ability to recognize His voice speaking to you in the moment of the situation. It is listening for Him daily. What He told you yesterday does not apply for today; what He told you even an hour ago might not be for now. What is He saying now?

Reflection Questions
For Chapter 3

What do you think it means to "have dominion" over the earth?

_____

_____

_____

Why is it important for us to understand that God wants us to have a relationship with Him?

_____

_____

_____

What does this statement mean to you? *The Holy Spirit will never do for us what we can do for ourselves.*

_____

_____

_____

What does having a "religious mindset" mean?

_____

_____

_____

Words to Know
Before Reading Chapter 4

Parable—A type of story that explains spiritual concepts and eternal truths through examples from nature or everyday life so they can be easily understood

Word of knowledge—The Holy Spirit reveals something that has happened in the past or is happening in the present. The person giving a word of knowledge would have no other way of knowing this information other than through the Holy Spirit.

Word of wisdom—The supernatural revelation by the Holy Spirit concerning the future plans and purposes of God

Discernment of spirits—The ability to perceive and distinguish between the Holy Spirit, demonic spirits, and the human spirit

The nine spiritual gifts—Supernatural gifts that are demonstrated by the Holy Spirit through Spirit-filled Christians for the profit of all. First Corinthians 12:8-10 lists them as the word of wisdom, the word of knowledge, faith, healings, the working of miracles, prophecy, discerning of spirits, different kinds of tongues, and the interpretation of tongues.

4

Ways the Holy Spirit Speaks to Us

IN THE NEW TESTAMENT, Jesus sent the Comforter, who is the Holy Spirit. Now His Spirit is in us and communicates with our spirit.

Holy Spirit can speak to us in many ways. He can speak through the Word. He can send us dreams or visions. He can also speak to our spirits. We can receive a word of knowledge or wisdom from Him. And we can receive discernment. Songs we listen to and books we are drawn to read are also ways Holy Spirit speaks to us. He speaks to us through nature, through art, and through other people. Any time you feel yourself stirred by something you see or hear or sense, ask the Holy Spirit what He is saying.

He speaks to both Christians and non-Christians. If a non-believer hears Father's voice (such as in Acts 10 when He spoke to Cornelius, who was not yet saved), how much more shall a Christian hear Him? If Father spoke to men who were not Christians, surely He will speak to His own children.

How do we always know He is the one who is communicating with us? What He says will bear witness with our spirit and align with His Word.

For as many as are led by the Spirit of God, they are the sons of God. For ye have not received the spirit of bondage again to fear; but ye have received the Spirit of adoption, whereby we cry, Abba, Father. The Spirit itself beareth witness with our spirit, that we are the children of God.

ROMANS 8:14-16

The most common way Holy Spirit speaks to us is through **His Word**. In the Gospels, we learn that Jesus spoke to man through parables.

I will open my mouth in a parable (in instruction by numerous examples); I will utter dark sayings of old [that hide important truth].

PSALMS 78:2 AMPC

The Bible itself is Father's voice on paper to speak life, clarity, direction, and instruction into us. Even if we never develop an ear to recognize His voice, we will always have the number one method of knowing His will by His written Word. Isn't that a comforting thought?

When the Holy Spirit chooses to speak to us, it always comes into alignment with the Word. The Father bound Himself to His Word. The Word is always our safety net for being able to discern what is of the Lord and what is not. That is the first and foremost way to know Father's will. His Word and His will are one. That is the reason we should always be in the Word!

Did you ever feel as though the Holy Spirit gave you a word in a dream or a vision? He uses **dreams and visions** as a way to communicate. In the Old Testament, the Lord primarily spoke to people in dreams and visions because they didn't have the Holy Spirit in them. Jesus had not yet come or been resurrected, so the Holy Spirit was sent in Jesus's place (John 14:26).

And he said "Hear now my words, if there be a prophet among you, I the Lord will make myself known unto him in a vision, and will speak unto him in a dream."

NUMBERS 12:6

There are many examples in the Bible of people having dreams from the Lord. In Old Testament times, it was easier for God to minister to man through dreams because the Spirit of God didn't yet dwell within man. Jesus had not yet died on the cross and risen again. The

Spirit of the Lord came upon them from time to time but didn't dwell within them. Dreams were so common or strong in those days that when Jacob's son Joseph told his brothers about his dream, they believed it so strongly they threw him in a pit to stop his dream from coming to pass. We know if it is a God-given dream, it will come to pass as it did for Joseph.

Here's an example of a vision in the New Testament:

There was a certain man in Caesarea called Cornelius, a centurion of what was called the Italian Regiment, a devout man and one who feared God with all his household, who gave alms generously to the people, and prayed to God always.
About the ninth hour of the day he saw clearly in a vision an angel of God coming in and saying to him, "Cornelius!"
And when he observed him, he was afraid, and said, "What is it, lord?"
So he said to him, "Your prayers and your alms have come up for a memorial before God.
Now send men to Joppa, and send for Simon whose surname is Peter. He is lodging with Simon, a tanner, whose house is by the sea.
He will tell you what you must do." And when the angel who spoke to him had departed, Cornelius called

*two of his household servants and a devout soldier
from among those who waited on him continually. So
when he had explained all these things to them,
he sent them to Joppa.*

ACTS 10:1-8 NKJV

We can see that Cornelius, a man who was precious in the sight of God, gave much money or alms to God's people and praised God always. The Lord appeared to him in a vision and gave him a word of knowledge about the location of Peter and also the street address. He also gave him the name of the man who owned the house, his occupation, and what city he lived in. All of this was told to him in a vision.

God will always do whatever He can to reach us if we are hungry enough for the things of God. If you read on in Acts 10, the Lord also gave Peter a vision that led him to go with the men who were sent to his door so salvation could come to Cornelius's household.

Visions and dreams happen even in today's times. I had a vision at home in my bed. I saw a person standing at the altar talking to the minister. I heard what the man was saying to the minister, and what he said was false. I felt I was supposed to call the person I saw speaking to the minister. When I questioned him about the false-hood, he was quick to anger. He was certain that some-one from the church had heard him and told me. It was a vision given to me by God. You, too, can have visions given to you by God.

There are nine spiritual gifts (1 Corinthians 12) given to the body of Christ. Three of them are called the revelation gifts. They are a word of wisdom, a word of knowledge, and the discerning of spirits. A **word of wisdom** always reaches into the future to reveal the plans and purposes of God. Sometimes we call this prophecy, but prophecy in this sense is not foretelling the future. Prophecy is the gift of speaking forth God's messages, focused on building up, encouraging, and comforting either individuals or the body of Christ.

A **word of knowledge** is a divinely inspired message that reveals something from the past or present that is unknown to the messenger but is known to the receiver. It is God's way of showing the person the message is from God.

A word of knowledge is God's way of showing the person the message is from God.

God speaks to us through people who teach, preach, sing, pray, or give us a word of prophecy, knowledge, or wisdom. It is important to know God loves us so much that many times He tells others to speak to us through these gifts. You know the person speaking is hearing from the Holy Spirit when they share something from your past or your present that is known to you but not familiar to the person giving the word.

Often, Holy Spirit sends a word of knowledge to someone to give to you. Or, if you have learned to listen for words from Holy Spirit, you'll receive the message directly. In Acts 14:9 Paul perceived that a man had the faith to be healed. Here, the Scripture used the term *perceived*. But many times, the Holy Spirit gives us a word of knowledge, which is knowing something that is revealed to us that has happened in the past or is happening now, in the present. Paul had a word of knowledge that this man had enough faith to be healed.

And there sat a certain man at Lystra,
impotent in his feet,
being a cripple from his mother's womb,
who never had walked:
The same heard Paul speak: who steadfastly
beholding him, and perceiving that
he had faith to be healed, Said with a loud voice,
"Stand upright on thy feet."
And he leaped and walked.

ACTS 14: 8-10

We can find these instances in the Bible, but WE can receive words of knowledge, too! I was on a mission trip in Mexico in the 1990's, and the people we were with locked their keys in the car. They asked me if I had a revelation of how to open the car.

They were not familiar with being filled with the Holy Spirit. They were fascinated with the gift of the word of knowledge, although they didn't believe the Holy Spirit spoke to man today other than through the written Word of God. They asked me what the Holy Spirit was saying to me.

I asked the Holy Spirit, under my breath, to speak to me and give me a word of knowledge about how to open the car so these men would believe that He speaks to men today. The Holy Spirit told me to walk around to the other side of the car. When I did, He said to look at the key insert. It was slightly turned to the left. He then told me to insert another key and turn it to the left.

I asked the men if anyone had a key. They all chuckled and reminded me the key was in the vehicle. I asked them again if any of them had a key—any type of key. One of them passed a key to me and told me that it wasn't a car key. I inserted the key into the keyhole, turned it left, and the door opened! They were all shocked. They were in disbelief and asked me several times how I knew how to unlock it.

I knew how to open the car by the unction of the Holy Spirit. When I told them that the Holy Spirit told me what to do and I simply obeyed, they laughed until they cried! They just couldn't believe in the supernatural.

If you don't believe in the supernatural, it can't work for you! Jesus said according to your faith or belief it will be done to you (Matthew 9:29).

> *"But ye have an unction from the Holy One,*
> *and ye know all things."*

1 JOHN 2:20

The Holy Spirit also sends **words of wisdom** to us. A word of wisdom means the Holy Spirit is revealing what will happen in the future. He can send a word of wisdom to someone who shares it with us, or He can send a word of wisdom directly to us.

Here is another time that Paul perceived, but this time it was a word of wisdom.

> *Much time had been lost, and sailing had already*
> *become dangerous because by now it was after the*
> *Day of Atonement. So Paul warned them, "Men, I can*
> *see that our voyage is going to be disastrous*
> *and bring great loss to ship and cargo,*
> *and to our own lives also."*

ACTS 27:9-10 NIV

They didn't heed Apostle Paul's warning, and in verses 21-26, he spoke another word of wisdom to which they did listen. Apostle Paul revealed these revelations to the captain of the ship. He was a prisoner of the ship, yet he took charge of it through and by a word from the Holy Spirit. Had Paul not listened for the voice of the Holy Spirit, things would have turned out much differently for the ship and all those aboard!

As I mentioned earlier, a word of wisdom always reaches into the future.

I was given a word of wisdom when I was working with Minister Alphonso Bailey at the New Castle, Indiana Correctional Center. I was teaching a group of men, and suddenly, the Holy Spirit told me a certain gentleman was going to get out early. I wrestled with whether I should tell him or keep it to myself. I stopped preaching and shared with him the word I was given. He told me that I must be mistaken because he had many more years to go. I told him that my word came from the Holy Spirit. Within three weeks, I received a call from Minister Alphonso to let me know that the gentleman had been released early!

A word of wisdom always reaches into the future.

Sometimes we call this prophecy. I had a man prophesy over me when I was a young Christian. He told me I was going to travel all over the world carrying the Gospel. It was difficult for me to see how God was going to send me around the world when I couldn't read and had little to no money. But I knew what he was saying was true because he told me the prayer I had just prayed before he pointed me out. I knew it had to be the Lord who told him my prayer. That was a word of knowledge about something that had just happened, which enabled me to believe the rest, which was a word of wisdom about the future.

Music is another way the Holy Spirit speaks to us. We know that music is in heaven because the angels sing. There are many scriptures about music. David praised the Lord and worshipped through his songs and musical instruments. We know music cuts across every nationality, language, race, and barrier.

Music is vital to the soul of man.

Every man's soul loves music. Music is vital to the soul of man. The number one way to reach a young person is through music. There is something so spiritual and stirring about it. The Holy Spirit may speak to us through the lyrics of a song. The Word tells us that Jesus Himself sings over us.

The Lord your God in your midst,
The Mighty One, will save;
He will rejoice over you with gladness,
He will quiet you with His love,
He will rejoice over you with singing.
ZEPHANIAH 3:17 NKJV

And **books**—the Holy Spirit can speak to us through books. What's the number one book in the world through which He speaks to us? The Bible!

There are many, many books written about the Word of God and about life from many perspectives. It is important to understand that God lives within man. And He gives people insight and wisdom about many different subjects that deal with spiritual as well as natural subjects. Where would the world be today without books?

All the ways Holy Spirit uses to speak to us come from a place of faith. We must believe we can be accessible and available for each way the Father chooses to speak to us. We must make time to listen to and read His Word. Faith comes by hearing the Word of God (Romans 10:17). The more of the Word we take in and comprehend, the stronger we grow in faith. Hebrews 11:6 says that if we are going to please God, it is through and by faith. God rewards those who seek Him by faith. And by faith, we will learn to hear what the Holy Spirit wants to tell us!

Reflection Questions
For Chapter 4

Name three ways the Holy Spirit can speak to you.

_____

_____

_____

What is the difference between a word of knowledge and a word of wisdom?

_____

_____

_____

Has there ever been a time when you felt the Holy Spirit spoke to you?

_____

_____

_____

Why is it so important to listen for the Holy Spirit?

_____

_____

_____

5

Why It Is Important to Hear the Voice of the Holy Spirit

I AM JUST A REGULAR GUY. I'm Johnnie Blount. God made me just the same as He made you. I started as a "baby Christian" the same as everyone else. But I have a passion to know Holy Spirit. I have a hunger to understand how and when He talks to me and what I need to do about it.

This chapter is about the importance of listening for the voice of the Holy Spirit. I'll also share some personal experiences of how my life changed when I listened to the Holy Spirit. I'm not the only one with whom He talks; however, I have had some powerful things happen in my life because I DID listen and obey.

When I think about all of the tragedies that take place in the world and especially in the body of Christ, I often wonder if the Father tried to communicate a warning to us before these disasters took place. I wonder if we were so busy reading the Bible from our denominational perspectives (religion and tradition) that we didn't hear the Lord. Was our denomination speaking louder than the Father?

The Word says in Mark 7:13 that men's traditions cause the Word of God to have no effect. The meaning behind that verse? The religious and traditional beliefs we've been taught from generation to generation cause the Word of God to not work for us.

One of those beliefs is that the Spirit of the Lord does not speak to men today. When we hear people say the Holy Spirit spoke to them, we dismiss what they say. Or when the Holy Spirit speaks to us, we don't recognize His voice because we don't believe He is speaking today.

We must be careful not to be snared by religious or traditional rules and procedures.

What I want you to understand is that when you submit to a denomination, you may limit yourself to how, when, and where God speaks to you.

We must be careful not to be snared by religious or traditional rules and procedures. This is one of the reasons you often hear me speak about division coming from the enemy, because we all need each other, not religious practice.

Jesus made the following statement to point out how the world deals better with one another than members of the church do: "So the master commended the unjust steward because he had dealt shrewdly. For the sons of this world are more shrewd in their generation than the sons of light" (Luke 16:8 NKJV).

"The sons of this world are more shrewd in their generation than the sons of light."

We have the Holy Spirit living within us, and the "sons of this world" have demons, yet they deal more wisely in life than we do because the enemy has blinded our minds through religion.

The United States military has members from every walk of life and nationality. They are fighting side by side for one common cause. It is not important what denomination they come from, whether they were baptized in the name of the Father, Son, and Holy Spirit, or whether they were baptized in Jesus only. Maybe they were sprinkled or dipped. Some have had communion every week. Some once a month. Some speak in tongues, and some have their own different prayer language. But none of these things separates them from being able to serve and fulfill their purpose in the United States military. The only way you can tell they are American citizens is by the uniform they wear.

When my son Johnnie graduated from boot camp, we attended his graduation at San Antonio Air Force

Base, and I was amazed at the different nationalities of people who graduated with him. There were so many different nationalities that I asked him how he would know who his enemies were and who his friends were.

He said, "We all have two things in common, Dad. We have the same uniform and the same language. We all speak English."

That is the way we should be known as believers. We should all speak the same language and wear the same uniform—the Word—rather than the doctrines of religious beliefs.

> *The Lord said, If as one people*
> *speaking the same language*
> *they have begun to do this,*
> *then nothing they plan to do*
> *will be impossible for them.*
>
> GENESIS 1:6

The US military knows you can't let your religious views hinder you from doing what is constitutional. For us, we can't let our religious views hinder us from being the Word.

If we can identify our Father's voice, then it is very possible He may forewarn us so we can avoid many difficulties. When my son David played college football, he told me that when he was playing in the heat of the battle on the field, he could hear my voice over all the other people shouting and cheering. He was able to recognize my voice because we have a relationship. We have spent a lot of time together. He knows the love I have for him. In the same way, that is why it's important to recognize our Father when He speaks to us. Jesus always said, "I only do what I hear my Father say." Jesus's desire and passion was to hear and obey. The Word tells us Jesus is our example.

It is important to hear the voice of our Father because He loves us and we love Him. If we don't hear our Father's voice, then how do we know how we're doing or what He needs us to do today? Our Father's will is our command. Whatever He so desires, our desire should be to fulfill it. The only way we can fulfill His desire is to hear His voice. Jesus had to hear the Father's voice in order to fulfill His purpose.

Don't you believe that I am in the Father,
and that the Father is in me? The words I say to you
I do not speak on my own authority.
Rather, it is the Father, living in me,
who is doing his work.
JOHN 14:10 NIV

Jesus could only fulfill the purpose of His Father by being able to recognize His Father's voice. How can we fulfill our purpose if we don't recognize the voice of the Father or the Holy Spirit?

Back to my son David. He mostly played defensive end, and his job was to turn the play to the inside and not allow the running back to run around the end. David had to cross the line and turn and face the quarterback so the play would turn and go up the middle where there were six or seven others who could stop the play. The offensive players who blocked my son were four to six inches taller and outweighed him by up to 100 pounds or more. They were so big that David couldn't see around them, and this blocked his view to recognize the play was coming his way. I would yell, "He's coming, David, he's coming!" And this would warn him they were trying to come by him. So, he was able to make the adjustment to stop the play.

If we don't recognize the voice of the Father, the enemy can have his way with us.

I give you this example because this is the same way the Father tries to warn us that the enemy is coming. If we don't recognize the voice of the Father, the enemy can have his way with us. Then, we may think it was the Father's will. The most tragic thing is not what happened, but that we didn't recognize our Father's voice because we haven't yet built a personal relationship with Him.

You may believe that because your parents, the priest, or the pastor know the Father, you are okay. But

YOU need to know your Father for yourself. It is important for us to remember our heavenly Father has no grandchildren. He only has children. We are all His children. In the Kingdom, we were all begotten by the Word of God. This is what we call being born the second time or "born again." God has no grandchildren because we are all brothers and sisters in the Lord.

In Judges 4:4, Deborah was the third prophetess recorded in the Bible, and she was a judge over Israel. She led Israel into battle. Barak was the general, and he wouldn't go to battle without Deborah because he knew she heard from the Lord. Judges 4:6 shows us clearly that Deborah was a prophetess because she knew the Lord had told Barak to go into battle. She knew the Lord had told Barak how many soldiers to take. She had also been told that the Lord told Barak He would deliver the Canaanites into his hand.

It was important for her to hear God's voice to fulfill the will and purpose God had for the children of Israel. The whole nation of Israel was delivered because Deborah recognized the voice of the Lord, and when she told Barak and his army, they obeyed. What a powerful example of listening to the Holy Spirit!

One Saturday, while I was at work in the coal mine, the Holy Spirit told me to take my one-year-old son Thomas to the doctor. I thought to myself, he must be sick. When I arrived home that afternoon, I asked my wife, Donis, how Thomas was doing. She told me he was fine and she had just laid him down to take a nap.

I told her what the Lord said. She told me the doctor's office was closed. We decided to wait until Monday to take him. But again, the Holy Spirit spoke to me and said, "No! Take him today."

Donis told me I would have to take him to the emergency room. It made no sense to me to carry a healthy child to the emergency room when there was no emergency. Donis asked me what I was going to tell them. I really didn't know. She stayed home with our other sons, Johnnie and David. Sometimes when you hear the voice of the Lord, you have to go along and alone.

I took Thomas to the Henderson Hospital emergency room, and the doctor asked me what was wrong with him. I told him I didn't know. I said maybe he had a cold. The doctor looked at me as if I were confused, and then he took Thomas. Three hours and three doctors later, they came back with test results. Thomas had pneumonia in one lung, and it had started to infect the other lung. The doctor said if Thomas had gone to sleep that night, he might not have awakened the next day. They kept him in the hospital for eight days. It was an eye-opening experience. What if I had dismissed this word from the Holy Spirit? The reason the Lord spoke a word of knowledge to me about taking Thomas to the doctor was to save his life! If I had not obeyed the voice of the

Holy Spirit, there is a strong possibility we wouldn't have Thomas or his three children today.

I used to pastor two churches at the same time. One church was in Morganfield, Kentucky and the other one in Hartford, Kentucky. I also worked the night shift full time in the coal mine. One night, while I was driving the two-hour commute home from the Hartford church to Morganfield, the Holy Spirit told me to stop by the home of one of my church members. It was already 9 p.m., and it was a two-hour drive. My scheduled work time was 11 p.m. On Bible study nights, my boss did allow me to come in a little bit later, but I didn't want to take advantage of that. When I got to Morganfield, Holy Spirit told me again to stop. But I was focused on getting ready for work.

I got home and put on my mining clothes. Donis told me she needed to talk to me about something, and we talked longer than I had planned. When I finally left for work, I intended to stop by my church member's house on the way, but time was too short, so I decided to stop in the morning. I went on to work.

At 2:30 a.m., my boss came to get me. He told me I had to go home because there was an emergency. It took an hour to get outside of the mine and call home. Donis told me that one of our members had passed away during the night. Her passing occurred at the same time the Holy Spirit told me to stop there. Three times, Holy

Spirit told me. Three times, I put it off. Decades later, it is still hard for me to pass by that house. It took me years to overcome the "what if." Friends, that is why it is so important to hear the voice of the Lord and obey. It is not enough to just recognize His voice. It is paramount to also obey promptly.

Another time I received a word from Holy Spirit was when my second son, David, was born. Donis had problems with her blood pressure rising during labor. The doctor was concerned about her health. He took the forceps and pulled David from her womb. She had been pushing for hours. When they took her to the recovery room, she said, "Blount, I'm hurting." When she said that, I felt an unction in my spirit. I heard something in her voice I had never heard before. I went to find the doctor, who was stepping into the elevator. I heard the Holy Spirit tell me to not let him get on the elevator.

I told the doctor about her pain. He said that it was because she just delivered an eight-pound-three-ounce-twenty-one-inch son. He continued to get on the elevator. I asked him again with more urgency to come and see her. He insisted he had given her some sleeping medication and medication for pain, and she would be fine.

Before the elevator door could close, I reached out my hand and grabbed him by his necktie to gently pull him off the elevator. He didn't want to come, but I encouraged him by pulling his tie a little harder. When he stepped off the elevator, I continued to hold his necktie as we walked down the hall. He slapped it out of my hand. The nurses were concerned about me pulling him by his tie. He assured them he was okay.

When we went into Donis's room, he pulled the covers back to examine her. His face dropped as if he had seen a ghost. He looked at the nurses standing there (because of the necktie pulling), and he shouted for them to get to the operating room now! He told them how many pints of blood to order stat and to get Donis to the operating room immediately! One of the nurses asked him who was going to perform the surgery, and he yelled that he was. A short time later, he returned and said that in another minute or two Donis would have died. She had ruptured an artery while she was pushing. He thanked me for being diligent in pursuing him.

I could have had two sons with no mother. I would have had no wife and no Thomas or Donise, our last two children, if I had not obeyed the voice of the Holy Spirit.

Listening for and to the voice of the Holy Spirit is so important. We must be diligent.

Reflection Questions
From Chapter 5

Why is it important to do what the Holy Spirit nudges us to do?

_____

_____

_____

Have you ever heard the Holy Spirit talk to you?

_____

_____

_____

What are some ways we can check ourselves to make sure it is really Him?

_____

_____

_____

What things have happened in your life that could have ended in a more positive way had you listened and obeyed the Holy Spirit's instruction?

_____

_____

_____

Words to Know
Before Reading Chapter 6

Faith—Hebrews 11:1 AMP describes faith as the proof of what is hoped for that is not yet seen and perceiving as real fact what is not revealed to the senses.

In agreement—Having harmony of opinion; the state of being in one accord

Supernatural—Beyond what is usual or normal, especially in a way that seems to defy the laws of nature; a spiritual existence beyond our natural abilities

Baptism of the Holy Spirit—(not the same as water Baptism) A supernatural, life-transforming experience of the love of God the Father poured into one's heart by the Holy Spirit, received through a surrender to the lordship of Jesus Christ, to give us greater ability to access the power of God and deeper intimacy with Him. It is usually evidenced by speaking in tongues. The apostles received the Baptism of the Holy Spirit in the Upper Room at Pentecost, when the Holy Spirit fell on them with power. The purpose of the Baptism of the Holy Spirit is to empower and embolden the believer to witness to the world the resurrection power and love of Jesus Christ and to expand His Kingdom through the supernatural gifts of the Holy Spirit.

6

Faith

HEARING THE HOLY SPIRIT speak to you requires faith. And faith must be built. Faith comes by hearing and doing the Word. James 1:23-25 tells us to be a *doer*, not just a *hearer*. By being a doer of the Word, we build faith.

If we stop exercising faith, it will shrink and eventually dissolve. Isn't that the way it is with anything? When you stop practicing football drills, you will have difficulty remembering them. When you quit playing the piano daily, the songs you memorized will begin to fade.

If you want your faith to grow, you must use it. You can't just read it and hear it; you must apply it! How much the Word lives in you determines the amount of faith you have available to use. If the Word does not live in you, you can't use it to access faith. The more you practice faith, the more your faith grows! It is of the utmost importance for us to realize that our Father wants us to recognize His voice. You don't have to beg Him to talk to you. He will. He doesn't just want to talk TO you. He wants to talk WITH you. And He wants to talk THROUGH you to others.

We must learn how to pray. We talk to Him when we pray, but too often we don't listen for Him to respond. Many times, when we are praying, we go into warfare against God by demanding Him to do things He has already finished from the foundation of the world.

His divine power hath given unto us all things
that pertain unto life and godliness,
through the knowledge of Him
that hath called us to glory and virtue.

2 PETER 1:3 KJ21

Prayer is one of the best ways to deepen our faith with God. God is not our obstacle. He is not our enemy. He is Father, and He has already provided whatever we are asking of Him. We don't need to command or demand or beg Him to do anything. It is done.

When you understand the Word and that what you ask of Him was finished from the foundation of the world, it will change the way you approach Him. When you understand this is a finished work—that Father is not *working on* but *has already completed*—it will also change the way you think and feel. He has already taken His seat and is at rest. His desire is for us to come into agreement with Him. If you are not in agreement with

His Word or His will, you are steadily begging (praying) for Him to heal you when you are already healed.

We must learn to believe what the Word says and SAY what the Word says even though we may not understand the Word or feel as if what we're saying is true. Our feelings are not always accurate, but the Word is. When we comprehend that what we ask for is finished, then everything we ask of the Father just needs to be a prayer of thanks. We can simply say, "Thank you, Father, that I am healed by the stripes of Jesus."

According to Mark 11:22-23, we can say to our mountain, our infirmity, or our obstacle, "You are trespassing. I am a temple of the Living God. I am a tabernacle, a place where God lives. I receive His Word that He sent to heal and deliver me from my own destruction."

If I bring forth to Him a prayer about healing my diabetes or high blood pressure or any kind of suffering, His Word, according to Psalm 107:20, tells me He has healed me and delivered me from my own destruction, whether it be financial, emotional, spiritual, relational, or situational.

All I need to do is properly apply the Word to my mountain, circumstances, and challenges. This mountain standing before me is there to challenge my faith.

James says our faith is on trial. I know and understand that God's Word says that I am whole, healed, delivered, prosperous, and merry. Now I must bring myself to believe what the Word says. If I confess it with my mouth and believe it in my heart and do not doubt, then I am in agreement with His Word, and whatever I am in agreement with has already come to pass in my life.

The physical world will deceive you. It will trick you!

Holy Spirit is telling us that our adverse circumstances and situations are lying to us. The lie is anything that goes against the Word of God. Second Corinthians 10:5 tells us to "cast down vain imaginations."

This is why we need to exercise our faith! We need to walk by faith and not by sight. The physical world will deceive you. It will trick you! Everything you can see, touch, feel, and smell was created first in the spiritual realm and then manifested in the physical realm.

You can change your physical circumstances by going into the spiritual arena and changing it. What you have in your hands today came out of your mind and out of your mouth. It was born in the spiritual realm before it manifested itself in the physical realm. That is why the Word says whatever you permit on earth, heaven will permit.

Father is not in the driver's seat. You are. He has put you in the driver's seat. Father is not going to deliver you from anything because He has already delivered you from all things. That is what salvation is. It is deliverance. Salvation is victory, prosperity, health, righteousness, peace, and joy. So, when you receive Christ, this is all in the package.

When you ask Him for things, He is telling you the answer is in the Word. That is why we must read the Word daily so we can comprehend our salvation. The more you read the Word, the more you will comprehend who your Father is, who you are, and what He has done for you.

I speak to people every week who tell me they have been reading their Bible twenty years or longer and are still praying for healing, money, and salvation for their family. BUT they remain in agreement with what they see and their circumstances. With their words, they are still creating a world they don't want. They talk, sing, believe, think, and meditate on what they don't want and then pray that God will change their world. You can't change your world until you change your thinking and your speech to line up with what the Word says!

Beloved, now are we the sons of God,
and it doth not yet appear what we shall be:
but we know that, when he shall appear,
we shall be like him;
for we shall see him as he is.
1 JOHN 3:2

Once you really read the Word, you will see time and time again how the Lord has already healed you and delivered you. It is already done. That is why we need to ask the Holy Spirit to open our eyes. Jesus said many times, "Those who have ears to hear, let them hear. Those who have eyes to see, let them see."

Faith believes what it doesn't understand, what it can't see with natural eyes, and what it can't hear with natural ears.

Our traditions, denominations, and culture have shaped our beliefs. It is hard to step outside of what we already know to believe something we don't know. That is what faith is, my friend, in a nutshell. Faith believes what it doesn't understand, what it can't see with natural eyes, and what it can't hear with natural ears.

So hold fast to your confession. Whose report shall you believe? God has chosen us—not that we have chosen Him. He sent His Word and delivered us. We are the sons of the Living God. We are more than conquerors through Christ Jesus. We can do all things through Christ who strengthens us (Philippians 4:13). We do have and operate with the mind of Christ.

Let this mind be in you, which was also in Christ Jesus.
PHILIPPIANS 2:5

Jesus has become our wisdom. There is nothing we can't accomplish.

Jesus said unto him, if thou canst believe,
all things are possible to him that believeth.

MARK 9:23

Hearing God's voice is one thing. But operating in the supernatural is another. In 1 Corinthians, chapters 12 and 14, Paul talks about supernatural gifts. Many people desire to operate in the supernatural gifts, but they can't because they are not yet filled with the Holy Spirit. They believe that just because they are Christian, they can operate in the supernatural.

Many times, when I am ministering to people about the gifts, they think or believe this is natural wisdom or natural knowledge or natural faith. But in 1 Corinthians 12:1, Paul said these are spiritual gifts. To operate in this wisdom takes insight from the Holy Spirit. To operate in the nine spiritual gifts listed in 1 Corinthians 12:8-10, you must first receive the power of the Holy Spirit. "But you shall receive power when the Holy Spirit has come upon you" (Acts 1:8).

We can see here that no one can have the power without being filled with the Baptism of the Holy Spirit.

Once we become Christians, we need to take that next step to receive the Baptism of the Holy Spirit. Luke said, in Acts 1:8, "Then you shall have power." When

Jesus walked the earth, He functioned and operated in the nine spiritual gifts.

When you enter a church that does not believe Acts 1:8, you don't experience the supernatural. You can tell by the praise and worship. You can tell by the prayers that are prayed. And you can tell by the Word that comes forth. They may have the Spirit of God in them, but the power of God is not upon them. In the Gospel of Matthew, Jesus says that signs and wonders shall follow the preaching of the Word. That means the supernatural should follow the preaching of the Word. When Jesus spoke, He always had signs and wonders follow.

You can hear the voice of the Lord without being filled with the Baptism of the Holy Spirit, but you must be filled with the Baptism of the Holy Spirit to be able to operate in the supernatural gifts. It is God's desire for us to be filled with the Baptism of the Holy Spirit and to be able to operate in the supernatural gifts.

Reflection Questions
For Chapter 6

What do we need in order to be able to hear the Holy Spirit talk to us?

_____

_____

_____

What is one important way to deepen our faith?

_____

_____

_____

Why does Dr. Johnnie say, "What comes out of your mouth governs what you have in your life"?

_____

_____

_____

Words to Know
Before Reading Chapter 7

Affirmations—Quoting Scripture or speaking positive declarations by faith for a particular outcome

Confession—(As used in this chapter) Acknowledgment or declaration by positive affirmation

7

Confess the Word

CONFESS. CONFESSION. When most people think of those words, they think of admitting to something they have done wrong. *Susie confessed she committed the crime. Robert confessed he didn't read the chapter before taking the test.* While that is one way to use those words, in this chapter, *confess/confession* means to acknowledge with affirmation—to speak what you believe and profess it out loud.

In the last chapter, I talked about how important it is to have faith for you to be able to hear the Holy Spirit talk to you. We must also confess our faith AND confess the Word!

In order for the Word to come alive to us, it is important for us to not only confess the Word, but also to meditate on it to keep it in our heart. The Lord told Joshua to keep the Word in his mouth and in his heart (Joshua 1:8). Those who make confessions daily but don't meditate on the Word won't see the manifestation of it in their lives. This is clear all throughout the Bible. This is a principle that works for us or against us.

James 1:6-8 tells us a double-minded person receives nothing from the Lord. To be double-minded means to ponder one thing in your heart but speak another thing out of your mouth—to mix faith and doubt.

A double-minded person receives nothing from the Lord.

For example, I confess with my mouth that I am healed, but in my mind, I see myself dying. My mouth and my mind are saying two different things. They are not in agreement.

Confessing and meditating on the Word will produce results. Solomon reiterated this when he said, "My son, give attention to my words; incline your ear to my sayings" (Proverbs 4:20). To give attention to God's Word is to not let the Word depart from your eyes. Trials, adverse circumstances, or tribulations will try to take your eyes off of the Word and onto your troubles. That is why when we make our affirmations (confessions) we need to look upon them as well as speak them.

When the Lord tries to get faith to come alive in man, He works with the eye gate through words and pictures, the ear gate through hearing the Word, the mouth gate through affirmations, and the mind gate through meditation so He can get the Word into our spirit.

The following are some examples from the Word of how the Lord spoke and used the physical senses of the person to make his message clear.

For all the land which you see I will give to you
and your descendants forever.

GENESIS 13:15 AMP

Then He brought him outside and said,
"Look now toward heaven,
and count the stars
if you are able to number them."
And He said to him,
"So shall your descendants be."

GENESIS 15:5 NKJV

And the Lord said unto Joshua,
"See, I have given into thine hand Jericho,
and the king thereof
and the mighty men of valor."

JOSHUA 6:2 KJ21

Then the Lord put forth his hand,
and touched my mouth.
And the Lord said unto me,
Behold, I have put my words in thy mouth.
See, I have this day set thee over the nations
and over the kingdoms,

to root out, and to pull down,
and to destroy, and to throw down,
to build, and to plant.

JEREMIAH 1:9-10

It was important for Abraham, Joshua, and Jeremiah to see the promise in the spiritual realm and in the natural realm in order to believe it and receive it. We can see how important the gates of our senses are. You have to be able to see it and say it in order to receive it! Jesus taught this principle to His disciples.

I will give you the keys of the kingdom of heaven;
and whatever you bind
(declare to be improper and unlawful) on earth
must be what is already bound in heaven;
and whatever you loose (declare lawful)
on earth must be what is already loosed in heaven.

MATTHEW 16:19 AMPC

A key always represents our authority. We must use our affirmations (speaking the Word), which is our authority, to bring things out of the invisible realm into the visible. Jesus tells us that whatever we permit on the earth, heaven will permit. And whatever we deny on the earth, according to the Word, heaven will deny. Our blessing comes when our mouth is in agreement with the Word. Jesus Himself affirmed this:

"For by your words you will be justified,
and by your words you will be condemned."

MATTHEW 12:37 NKJV

Jesus's statement about our words means we are justified (made right) or condemned (pronounced guilty) here and now, on a daily basis, by what we speak out of our mouths. In the same way, Solomon, the wisest man who ever lived, said this about our words:

Death and life are in the power of the tongue:
and they that love it shall eat the fruit thereof.

PROVERBS 18:21

When you speak negatively, you bring death and condemnation upon yourself. But when you choose to speak positively, you call forth blessings into your life. This is a principle that operates in the earth and works for everyone! This is what Paul taught:

If you confess with your mouth the Lord Jesus
and believe in your heart
that God has raised Him from the dead,
you will be saved.

ROMANS 10:9 NKJV

What you confess with your mouth and believe in your heart comes to pass in your life. That principle works both positively and negatively. When you confess and believe in prosperity, you become prosperous. When you confess and believe sickness, you become sick.

Casting down imaginations,
and every high thing that exalteth itself
against the knowledge of God,
and bringing into captivity
every thought to the obedience of Christ ...

2 CORINTHIANS 10:5

Even our thoughts must line up with the Word if we want to have good success. There is an ancient proverb that says, "See no evil, hear no evil, speak no evil." Here is what the Word of God says about it:

Let no corrupt communication
proceed out of your mouth,
but that which is good to the use of edifying,
that it may minister grace unto the hearers.

EPHESIANS 4:29

He who walks righteously
and speaks uprightly,
He who despises the gain of oppressions,
Who gestures with his hands, refusing bribes,
Who stops his ears from hearing of bloodshed,
And shuts his eyes from seeing evil:

He will dwell on high;
His place of defense
will be the fortress of rocks;
Bread will be given him,
His water will be sure.

ISAIAH 33:15-16 NKJV

What you say shall and will come to pass. James 3:8 tells us that the tongue is full of deadly poison, and it will corrupt the whole body simply by speaking negative things out of our mouth. This is why it is important for us to put a guard on our tongue.

Then He said to them,
"Take heed what you hear.
With the same measure you use,
it will be measured to you;
and to you who hear, more will be given."

MARK 4:24 NKJV

We have two sets of ears. We have natural ears and spiritual ears. Most people hear only with their natural ears. But when Jesus speaks, He speaks to the spiritual ears. This is why He has spoken in the Word, "He who has ears to hear, let him hear." To those who can hear, He gives revelation, which is more insight into the supernatural or spiritual things of God.

My son, attend to my words;
incline thine ear unto my sayings.
Let them not depart from thine eyes;
keep them in the midst of thine heart.
For they are life unto those that find them,
and health to all their flesh.

PROVERBS 4:20-22

Solomon gave this wisdom to his son about keeping the Word before his eyes and in his heart. He was teaching him that the Word is precious and valuable because it is life, health, and prosperity. It will bring you peace to weather the stormy times of life. We know that Solomon was speaking of a spiritual ear because he said the Word itself is medicine to all those who find it.

Let the words of my mouth,
and the meditation of my heart,
be acceptable in thy sight, O Lord,
my strength, and my redeemer.

PSALM 19:14

Here we can see that David is saying to the Lord, "Let my thoughts and my words be according to Thy Word." David knew that within God's words are peace and eternal life. He understood that in order for things in his life to go well, his inner thoughts or meditation must be according to the Word also.

If you have been foolish in exalting yourself,
or if you have devised evil,
put your hand on your mouth.

PROVERBS 30:32 NKJV

Solomon understood that what a man thinks about will proceed from his mouth. He advised us to place our hands upon our mouths to refrain from speaking about anything negative or evil, because if we meditate on wrong things, we will speak wrong things, and speaking those things will bring them into existence.

"Brood of vipers! How can you, being evil,
speak good things? For out of the abundance
of the heart the mouth speaks.
A good man out of the good treasure of his heart
brings forth good things,
and an evil man out of the evil treasure
brings forth evil things.
But I say to you that for every idle word
men may speak, they will give account of it
in the day of judgment."

MATTHEW 12:34-36 NKJV

Jesus tells us that the words we speak come from our hearts. Our thinking or meditation on good or evil, over a period of time, by both speaking and meditating on it, will cause ideas and beliefs to drop into our hearts and become truth to us. That is why we hear people say foolish things, and we ask ourselves how in the world they could believe something like that. Their beliefs came from their thoughts.

We give an account daily of the words we speak. We are justified or condemned by our own words. We are justified when we come into agreement with the Word and declare what it says about our circumstances.

Romans 4:17 says, "Call those things that be not as though they were." Jesus said to speak to the mountain (negative circumstance or obstacle) to be removed and cast into the sea and it shall obey you (Mark 11:23). He said if you have faith as small as a mustard seed you shall say to the sycamore tree to be plucked up by the root and be planted in the sea and it shall obey you (Luke 17:6).

The Lord is trying to help us comprehend the importance of using the authority we have over our circumstances. He continually tells us to speak to our situation and it will obey us. In times of trouble, Jesus said for us to speak to trouble. We tell Jesus about our troubles, but He tells us to take our authority over our troubles by speaking life to them.

Don't tell the Word about your troubles; tell your troubles about the Word!

Reflection Questions
For Chapter 7

Why is it so important to constantly think about what comes out of your mouth?

_____

_____

_____

What does Scripture mean when it says we "have author-ity over our circumstances"?

_____

_____

_____

Write about something you are struggling with in your life that could be changed by the way you think and speak. Begin to think and speak about it with positivity and authority according to what the Word says about it.

_____

_____

_____

So What's Next?

HAVING A PERSONAL RELATIONSHIP with Holy Spirit changes lives. Reading the Word changes lives. Learning to listen for a Word from Holy Spirit changes lives.

- Read and meditate on the Word daily to become familiar with the character, voice, and will of the Father.

- Set aside time every day to quiet your mind and ask the Holy Spirit to increase your ability to hear Him.

- In every situation, exercise your spiritual eyes and ears and senses by asking Holy Spirit to show you the ways the Father is speaking to you.

- Weigh what you hear to discern if it aligns with the Word and the will of God.

- Obey and act on what the Holy Spirit tells you.

- Seek out and receive the Baptism of the Holy Spirit if you have not already received it.

My friends, I hope this book has helped you to recognize the voice of Holy Spirit and to be led by Him. I have no doubt that hearing the voice of Holy Spirit and doing what He asks of you will change your life. God bless you!

About the Author

A PROPHET AND VISIONARY, Dr. Johnnie Blount is known internationally for his ability to guide individuals to spiritual maturity and revelation of the Kingdom of God. He is a dynamic speaker and author who shares the message of the Kingdom Jesus came to reveal. Flowing in the gifts of the Holy Spirit, he serves others by ministering the power, love, grace, and truth in the Word of God.

Dr. Blount's mission is to empower the believer to walk in the possibilities, purpose, provision, and revelation of Kingdom principles. To accomplish this vision, he founded Be the Word Ministry and Be the Word Kingdom Academy. He writes, speaks, holds conferences, has a weekly online Bible study, and travels throughout the United States as well as internationally.

Dr. Blount has been ministering since he was fifteen years old. Throughout his many years of ministry, he has been a pastor, established three churches and two Bible colleges, and has led many mission trips. In ministering to the youth in Job Corps, he and his team led over 15,000 souls to salvation.

Dr. Johnnie and his wife, Donis, have been married since 1980 and have four children and eight grandchildren and counting. He can be contacted through his website: https://bethewordministry.com.

www.ingramcontent.com/pod-product-compliance
Lightning Source LLC
Chambersburg PA
CBHW051722090426
42738CB00010B/2037